Find Your WOW

How seeing the world differently might just save your mind.

Lucy Stone

Find Your WOW

First published 2023

Published by Wonderfield Publishing Ltd, 7 Chelsea Rd, Bath, BA1 3DU and under licence by Brown Dog Books, 10b Greenway Farm, Bath Rd, Wick, nr. Bath BS30 5RLL

ISBN printed book: 978-1-83952-653-4

Co-edited by Patrick Ubezio
Cover design by Andrew Prescott
Internal design by Andrew Easton
Illustrations © Lucy Stone

Printed and bound in the UK

This book is printed on FSC® certified paper

This book is for all of those who have made me say WOW, shared moments of WOW with me or taught me how to find WOW every day.

For Freddie, the biggest WOW of my life.

For my mum Maureen, dad Jim and brother Ian.

For Patrick, thank you for everything; the cups of tea, the road trips, the editing, the love and for being my WOW warrior.

For my friends who join me wearing sequins dancing in fields, GOAH, my allotment gang, schoolfriends (especially Sarah) and the ones who laugh and find WOW with me in the strangest of places.

For Barney, for all the walks and cwtches.

I love you all.

And finally, THANK YOU to the over 15,000 children who were the original inspiration for this book and I was lucky enough to find WOW with, as we practised mindfulness together in the classrooms. You taught me more than I could have ever taught you. To the wonderful, inspiring teachers I have been able to work alongside, especially Mrs Jo Bird. To my meditation crew who know who they are. And to Douglas, Frances, Melanie, Klaus, Suzy, Amy and others who helped me to get Find Your WOW out into the world.

Just WOW.

The elevator pitch:

As children we have a natural sense of awe and wonder of the world, as adults we lose it; this book helps you to get it back and Find Your WOW.

Contents

Contents

'*The pursuit of truth and beauty is a sphere of activity in which we are permitted to remain children all our lives.*'

– Albert Einstein

Chapter 1.

Introduction

Try and remember the last time you said WOW out loud? Can you remember what you were doing at the time? Where were you? Who were you with? How did you feel in that moment, and how long did that feeling last?

It might have taken you a moment or two to recall when that was.

You might not even remember a recent time when you've said WOW, so you instead recall one from your past. You might recount a memory where you were so struck by an experience, it stopped you in your tracks and is imprinted in your mind forever.

Now, rather than trying to recount one of the big WOWs from your life (those milestone moments), try to think of a smaller, simpler WOW, which surprised or inspired you. When you experienced something so incredible it took your breath away, you felt goosebumps and you were left feeling overcome with awe and wonder?

In these moments, **you have experienced WOW**.

Children say WOW a lot, certainly many more times in an average day than adults.

If you have ever walked with a young child, you've probably stopped to look at the cracks in the pavement to explore the insect world at your feet. Maybe you've experienced the delight on Christmas morning when children play with an empty cardboard box, as the (often expensive) toy you have just gifted them, lays redundant at its side. Perhaps you've lain on the grass alongside a youngster who shows you all the shapes they can see forming in the clouds above.

If you have experienced any of these things, you have **witnessed moments of WOW**.

Being an adult can be stressful, exhausting and boring. Much of daily life is filled with responsibilities, 'to do' lists, chores and admin. We are busy 'spinning plates' and multitasking our way to oblivion, the weekend or next holiday or retirement, with hardly a moment to breathe. Carving out any time for ourselves, let alone time for finding WOW might seem like an impossible task. Life was so much simpler when we were a child.

Are you ready for the bad news? It might not come as too much of a surprise, but research shows the average 21st-century adult is more stressed, has a shorter concentration span and has less connection with the natural world than at any other time in history.[1] Instead, many of us find ourselves for hours a day in a virtual, online world. We might feel as if we have 'seen everything before' as we rush from one appointment to the next, with little chance to stop and notice what is around us, with no time for ourselves. We might end up feeling just a little bit lost.

I am afraid the doom and gloom doesn't stop there. (I promise it gets more cheerful in a moment.) At the time of writing this book, we are emerging from a global pandemic, there is a war in Ukraine, and the world is facing difficult political, economic, environmental and population crises. Some of us are entering a new era of hybrid working, and the number of children and adults with diagnosed mental health conditions is higher than ever before. The word of the year for 2022 was 'Permacrisis' a never-ending spiral of doom, made worse by a continuous feed of mainstream and social media breaking news alerts.[2]

Many adults feel overwhelmed, an increasing number are burnt out, we might feel as if we have lost a sense of who we are, and almost all of us are just plain tired. The good news is that this book, set against this seemingly depressing backdrop, hopes to shed a little light and bring a positive new way of looking at life and the world. Perhaps it was never needed more.

My name is Lucy Stone. In my mid-thirties, I was juggling motherhood and a busy career, but felt anxious and exhausted. I had lost a sense of what I needed or wanted from life. After resigning from a busy agency where I was PR Director, I travelled to India to rest, recover and regain a sense of who I was. Whilst there I retrained as a yoga and meditation teacher.

That was seven years ago, and since then I have worked on the frontline of British classrooms, teaching meditation to over 15,000 primary school children. In parallel, I have taken my teaching from the classroom to the boardroom, and taught thousands of senior leaders, chief executives and managers in the corporate world.

I am in a unique position. After simultaneously teaching meditation to thousands of children, and adults, I have an unparalleled insight into how humans of differing ages approach learning a new skill, practising mindfulness and well, life in general.

When some of the corporate leaders found out about my other work teaching children, they were fascinated and asked, 'how on earth do you teach a four-year-old to meditate?' My answer to that question is that 'four-year-olds learn meditation quicker and easier than say, a 54-year-old chief executive.' This often started a debate as to why that might be, and we will explore these reasons in this book.

A child's young life is full of daily discovery, a world of imagination and moment to moment living. Every waking hour is spent learning, playing, feeling.

CHILDREN SAY WOW A LOT.

My two main observations, which have inspired this book are:

1. Perhaps surprisingly, children (especially those under ten years old) find mindfulness meditation easier to grasp than adults, and
2. The word WOW is more commonly heard in the classroom (and rarely in the boardroom)

Could there be a link between these two things?

After being asked so many times 'How do you teach a four-year-old to meditate?' I started to observe the children and adults in my sessions more closely. What did the children do that was different to the adults? Why did children master the skill so much easier? What is it about a child's approach to mindfulness (and maybe even life) which meant they 'got it' so much quicker than their older counterparts? I started to make a list.

I wrote a blog with the title '15 lessons I have learnt from teaching meditation to fifteen thousand children.' I listed 15 reasons why I thought children might find mindfulness meditation easier to grasp than adults, based purely on what I had observed during my years of teaching.

Since then, as the world has gone through a period of incredible change, I have reflected on those 15 observations, and in addition, researched the science and rationale on why children are naturally more mindful, and perhaps even, what we as adults can learn from them.

Originally, I thought this book was going to be about my observations. But as I dug deeper into academic research and started to understand more about the workings of the brain, I discovered there is something even more interesting at play.

I realised at the core of those 15 reasons was something new. Those observations were not only interesting to note on their own as an attitude towards learning and life, but also together they amounted to something much bigger. Suddenly, I had an incredible realisation of what children 'have' and we, as adults 'lose'.

As adults we lose our childlike awe and wonder
of the world, which can be captured by one word,
WOW. We have lost our WOW.
We are living most of our time in a WOW-less world,
and this is not doing us any good.
In fact, it might even be making us ill.

But the good news is (and I told you there was some) I have developed a way for you, for us all, to easily find WOW once again. Based on what those 15,000 children have shown and taught me over the years, I have created the building blocks on which we can live our life, which might just save our mind. As we will discover, finding WOW has consequences for our health, our well-being, our work, our relationships, our quality of life and our happiness.

Over the course of the book, I refer to the five pillars of WOW, which can help us rediscover what we as grown-ups commonly have lost, and children have in abundance: WOW. I developed these five pillars based on years of research, interviewing experts and through my experience of teaching mindfulness to thousands of children and adults.

This book is here to help you to once again, Find Your WOW.

THE FIVE PILLARS OF WOW ARE:
1. Being in the moment and fully present **(NOW)**
2. Letting go of distractions **(FOCUS)**
3. Accessing the state of flow **(FLOW)**

4. Silencing your inner critic or critical self **(EGO)**
5. Cultivating the conditions for WOW experiences **(WOW)**

These pillars will come up frequently throughout the book and each one provides the foundations and conditions that allow WOW to flourish. They are not mutually exclusive, nor do they have a particular order or hierarchy. But they are vital to our understanding of WOW, where and how to find it, and will provide guidance as you digest what you read in the forthcoming pages and reflect on your own life.

Now you might be sitting there thinking I really don't have a clue what you are talking about? What on earth do you mean by WOW? So, before much longer, it might be useful to define what I mean by the WOW experience and put a loose definition on what constitutes WOW.

Let's start with the dictionary definitions of WOW, where the word can be used in three different ways.

1. As an **exclamation**: WOW! This cake is delicious, please tell me the recipe.
2. A person or an object that is **very successful, attractive or pleasant**: The teacher is a real WOW with the students in the class.
3. To make someone feel **great excitement or admiration**: The film wowed audiences with its incredible special effects.

My definition of WOW brings these three examples together to take a new meaning.

First, history. WOW might sound like a modern word, but the Oxford English Dictionary traces its origins all the way back to 1513, when translator Gavin Douglas wrote in his English version of Virgil's Aeneid: 'Out on thir wanderand spiritis, **wow!** thow cryis.' By the end of the 1800s, WOW was in regular use by (mostly) English speakers, as an exclamation.[3]

By the start of the 20th century, this began to change. The 1920s and 1930s really were the decades of WOW and researchers who have studied the word's popularity over the last two centuries noticed its use really exploded in that time. In 1920, the word WOW was used as a noun; 'this orchestra is a WOW'. Four years later, the word is listed as a verb, you could 'WOW someone with a dazzling display' and by 1932, WOW was a specific technical term that refers to an audio distortion in which the frequency suddenly goes up and then down, making a 'WOW' sound.

The evolution of the word hasn't stopped over the last century. Once it became a written term, it was adopted across the globe and its simplicity is perhaps why it is so similar across a huge number of languages, like the Spanish guau, Korean 와우 (wau), Russian Вау (vau) but many more languages just use 'wow'.

Its simplicity, the sound the word makes when spoken and its multitude of uses might explain its popularity and continued use, but for the purposes of this book I am going to take a slightly different interpretation of its definition.

When I refer to WOW, I define it as a strong, positive emotional state where an experience goes beyond expectation, which has a lasting effect on the body and mind.

In Find Your WOW, there are two essential qualities of WOW. Firstly, there is an element of surprise. A moment of WOW is often a pleasant and unexpected experience. Secondly, what constitutes a moment of WOW is subjective and personal. During this book we will explore **what** constitutes a WOW experience and **how** to trigger more moments of WOW.

Throughout this book, you will come to understand why we do not say WOW as often as we did as children. There are a multitude of reasons for this, but also some sad and significant consequences of what happens when we stop saying WOW.

We spend more time worrying, and less time wondering about the world.

When I was researching for the book, I interviewed people about their most memorable WOW moments. I asked friends and family when the last time was, they had said 'WOW' with real meaning. You know, those moments of WOW which are spontaneous, the word just falls from your mouth, and you are completely in awe of something which has happened.

Some told me about a time they mastered a skill, like learning how to juggle or a new yoga pose. Some described experiences that stimulated their senses, like watching modern ballet, tasting incredible food or listening to a performance at a music concert. It is clear there are many ways to experience WOW.

In later chapters I will describe the detailed criteria of what makes up a moment of WOW, and how you can begin to cultivate the conditions to make way (and time) for more WOW in your everyday life. You'll also learn how WOW is connected to mindfulness and the state of flow (the pleasant sensation you feel when you are totally immersed in what you are doing, and your skills are in balance with the challenge you face).[4] You will also discover why children have an unfair advantage over adults when it comes to experiencing WOW.

My concept of WOW brings together a childlike view of the world, that is not to say immature, a mindset of curiosity, having a mindful approach to life and crucially, that all important sense of awe and wonder. In our ever-busy lives as adults, it might be hard to imagine having the time to rekindle this way of viewing the world. I want to reassure you that once you learn the technique for finding your WOW once again, not only could it become part of your life without you even noticing that you are doing it, but it might also help you to feel happier, have a greater connection to others, and improve your overall health and well-being in all areas of your life.

Sadly, I don't have a time machine, and I am not sure how many of us would want to start our lives all over again from childhood. But what I do have is a framework of how we can tap into and access a childlike version of ourselves and bring some of that curiosity, mindset and practice into our lives. Maybe if you learn how to (re)Find Your WOW, you might start to see the world a little differently, which might in turn help your mind, and maybe help others too. The fact that children use WOW in their everyday lives, not knowing how or why they are using this term, is inspirational. But you don't need to be a child, or even childlike to find WOW. Finding WOW needn't cost a penny and might be one of the best investments you'll ever make.

This book takes the lessons I have learnt from teaching and practising meditation, backed by scientific evidence and research which looks at what children 'have' and as adults we 'lose', and what might happen if we can get some WOW back. We examine more closely why children are such WOW-masters, and what we can learn from their outlook on life. We'll consider the importance of WOW for our health and well-being, and what happens if we live in a WOW-less world. And crucially, we will learn the framework to help you Find Your WOW, and how we can all find moments of WOW in our everyday, to reconnect with who we really are and feel the physical, mental and emotional benefits of WOW in our own life.

This book is for anyone who has watched a child play without inhibition, full of creativity, and longs to be in their shoes. For anyone who feels like they have lost their childlike sense of awe and wonder of the world and wants to get it back. This book will help you rediscover the joy in small things, to reconnect with who you really are and with what's important.

This book is about seeing life through new eyes, and to help you once again, Find Your WOW, which might just save your mind.

I hope you enjoy this journey of exploration.

This book is for you. Are you ready to Find Your WOW?

'Sometimes you will never know the value of a moment, until it becomes a memory.'

– Dr Seuss

Chapter 2.

We are living in a WOW-less world

Sometimes you might feel as if you are living in a WOW-less world, drowning in routine, feeling somehow disconnected and apathetic towards life around you.

The media and social media feeds us a diet of extremes with only the funniest, best, fastest, most evil, craziest, stupidest and the most beautiful ever making the cut. One of the saddest and starkest lessons we must eventually learn as adults is that (unless we take positive action) a lot of our life is routine and average, with occasional highs and lows to punctuate the mundane. Trying to live a well-balanced life whilst consuming the most extreme versions of everything can magnify our own 'averageness' and take its toll on even the most optimistic of souls.

Right now, the world is emerging from a pandemic, we are adjusting to a new hybrid world, reflecting on what's changed, and what life looks like for us now. At the same time, many of us are under increased financial pressures with the rise in the cost of living and energy bills. We are living in a fast-paced online-focussed world, with 24-hour rolling news and entertainment and everything is readily accessible. More content is produced in one day throughout the globe, than we can ever consume in our lifetime. So, in an ever-noisy landscape, how can any WOW ever cut through?

WOW-lessness is all around us; we are spending less and less time in nature, becoming more and more isolated in our virtual worlds, fewer and fewer opportunities for real life connections with fellow humans, our entertainment and social connections increasingly online, rather than real world. Although our planet and our life could be 'wonder-full', many of us might feel as if we are living in a WOW-less world.

Although I use the term 'WOW-less' with a little tongue-in-cheek, there are eight reasons I believe we are living in a WOW-less world:

1. WE ARE LIVING IN A STRESSFUL WORLD
In 2016, the World Health Organization announced that stress is the health epidemic for the 21st century. The effects of stress on the body and mind are well documented, and although we need a healthy dose of stress to survive and thrive, you can have too much of this good thing. Sometimes the balance can tip over where we begin to feel that our physical and mental health is affected. Our bodies were not designed to run on stress hormones such as adrenalin and cortisol, and the modern-day mind often suffers with their after-effects such as anxiety, trouble switching off at the

end of the day or sleeping, and a lack of drive or focus. The hangover of stress and anger can take around seven hours to leave the body, in the meantime, high levels of damaging cortisol are pumping around our body, doing no good at all.

During the pandemic, stress levels soared, and remain high, according to a 2022 international workforce and well-being mindset report,[1] the majority (73 per cent) of employees in the US and Western Europe rate their current stress levels as moderate or high and over a third state they are suffering symptoms of burnout. In the UK, it is reported that at least a quarter of people have diagnosed mental health problems.[2]

Whether we are experiencing the inevitable stress of everyday life, or suffering from specific mental health challenges, we can lack energy, lose interest in what is around us, become disconnected or withdrawn and our focus, productivity and motivation can decrease.

But the good news is there has been a lot of research on how exposure to 'awe' (or WOW) inducing experiences can help to relieve stress, which we will uncover in the coming chapters.

2. WE ARE LIVING IN A FILTERED WORLD

Over the past decade there has been an incredible rise in the popularity of social media, with filtered versions of people's lives filling our feeds. We can choose to be a part of the social media game, or leave it well alone, but most of us will be either directly or indirectly exposed to social media in some form.

We know the AI-tailored newsfeed, the filtered images, the short and snappy videos giving us a glimpse of the influencers' curated life, is not the whole story. But for too many of us, social media has a real and lasting effect. The natural inclination to compare our lives with others is too tempting, but as Theodore Roosevelt once said, 'comparison is the thief of joy'. The dopamine hit we get from refreshing our newsfeed has been likened to that of a gambling addict pulling the arm of the one arm bandit machines in the casino, the dopamine we feel when someone likes or retweets our post is all, quite simply, designed to be addictive.

We are encouraged to be 'the best version of ourselves', while many of us are running on empty.

The engineers who designed the 'like' button and 'never-ending' newsfeed have talked extensively about the 'guilt' they feel from the impact their seemingly simple design feature might have had on the world. Author Simon Sinek has called for age restrictions on social media as he believes it is causing untold damage to our young adults who are feeling 'fine' about everything, unable to find real joy (or WOW) in anything much at all.[3]

But while social media is likely here to stay, and can potentially dilute our WOW experiences, as you will discover in later chapters, perhaps it can also play a part in finding it too. It is important to set boundaries on what is healthy for you, and not rely on social media as your only source of WOW.

3. WE ARE LIVING IN A DISTRACTED WORLD

Over the past decade, there has been a decline in our human ability to focus. Our attention spans are becoming shorter and the number of adult and child diagnoses of neurodivergence, such as ADHD, is increasing.[4] In the United States between 2007 and 2016, adult diagnosis of ADHD was up by 123 per cent, outpacing the rate of increase in child and adolescent cases.[5] There is some indication that these numbers have continued to rise during the pandemic.[6]

As you might expect, there is a direct link between screen time and the ability to focus. A study[7] from 2019 revealed the global attention span was narrowing due to the amount of information we are presented with each day; we all have more things to focus on for shorter periods of time. The researchers stated that while social media plays its part in this shift, it is not all to blame as the trend for shortening attention spans began at least 100 years ago.

Content is increasing in volume, which exhausts our attention and our urge for 'newness' causes us to collectively switch between topics more regularly.[8] Many people have anecdotally reported this has worsened during and since the pandemic, where many of us were forced to increasingly rely on screens for school, work, social connection and running our day-to-day lives.

When distracted, we find it difficult to focus on the things that matter to us, at work, in relationships or in our personal and creative lives. Whether our distractions are external, such as phone notifications or internal such as thoughts and feelings, losing focus can cause frustration and anxiety, leaving us feeling unsatisfied and stressed.

It is not just the temptation of the dopamine hit from the online world which can cause distraction, when we lose focus, perhaps due to a notification on our phone, our state of flow is disrupted which in turn decreases productivity, creativity and even happiness.

4. WE ARE LOSING TOUCH WITH THE NATURAL WORLD
Humans are spending less time outdoors, specifically in nature, than we did in previous generations. As we will explore in later chapters, access and connection to the natural world is not only essential to our physical and mental well-being, but also one of the greatest providers of WOW, and we are limiting our access to these experiences. Children in school, spend most of their playtimes outside but a survey carried out in 2019 revealed that 50 per cent of adult Brits spend less than an hour in the open air each day, whereas 70 per cent want to spend more time outside. Particularly in the dark, winter months, we might struggle to spend any quality time in daylight during the working week, and over 56 per cent of humans live in urban environments and cities.[9]

Not spending enough time outside, particularly in nature, has a negative effect on our health. Research shows that when you spend more time outdoors it not only reduces anxiety and improves your mood, but the levels of the feel-good hormones (serotonin and dopamine) are increased within the body, which help you feel calmer and happier. Getting into nature is a complete tonic for the whole body and mind. The exercise is beneficial and being in green spaces sends a natural signal to the brain to slow down. Spending time in the fresh air can increase your endorphin levels, which helps to relieve pain or stress and boosts happiness. Sunlight is also a source of Vitamin D, which is essential for our overall health and well-being.

New research from the University of Tokyo in 2022 suggests the benefits of spending time in nature extends much further than previously thought.[10] And the ancient practice of forest bathing (known as Shinrin Yoku in Japan) is seeing a modern-day resurgence.

The number of young people and adults seeking support for their mental health is higher than ever before, at the same time many of us are feeling an increased sense of concern for the health of our planet. On the flip side, during the pandemic and lockdowns, many of us took time to positively connect and appreciate the natural world and have found joy in simple activities. We might have vowed never again to take for granted those small things which brought us pleasure, but as life picks up pace, it is increasingly difficult to make time.

5. WE ARE LIVING IN A BUSY WORLD

You might feel as if you are always busy and wear 'being busy' as a badge of honour. You ask a work colleague how they are as they make a cup of tea in the office kitchen, 'Busy' comes the often-deflated reply. The state of 'busyness' has become the norm. Many of us are stressed, overworked, exhausted, eating lunch at our desks (if at all), rushing from one appointment to the next, and before we know it, our day is over. We look forward to our weekends, until we finally reach our holidays and maybe, just maybe, take a break. When we are busy and stressed, we can struggle to focus, connect or engage with our day. We might not experience any emotions and instead feel like we are 'going through the motions'.

We might feel more 'Human Doing' than Human Being.

Research indicates that an individual's perceived level of busyness may be connected to their perception of their own self-worth as well as how others view their status. Being busy and productive are not the same thing. When we are busy and become over extended or overwhelmed this may lead to amongst other things, stress, anxiety, anger, loneliness, hopelessness and depression.

MULTITASKING IS THE CURSE OF THE MODERN WORLD.

As we will discover in later chapters, we are not built to multitask, as nice as it would be to do two things at once, neuroscience and countless studies show that the brain is simply not capable of paying full attention to more than one thing at a time. So many of us describe feeling like 'headless chickens' at times, rushing, chaotic, not efficient, but certainly, busy.

'We are amusing ourselves to death.'
– Neil Postman[11]

6. WE ARE LIVING IN A SCREEN-BASED WORLD

In the modern world, much of our entertainment, information and connection is via a screen. Whether that is watching a series on Netflix, listening to music or podcasts, gaming, social media, keeping in touch with people, accessing the internet, apps or even reading a book via a Kindle. We might even track our steps, stress levels and heart rate via a screen strapped to our wrist. For many people, the crossover of their work and personal online world is blurred. How many times have you intended to just read one work-related email but quickly checked social media, and ended up in an online black hole or found yourself doom scrolling?

Algorithms know us better than our loved ones do when it comes to choosing birthday presents, and AI can auto-remember our passwords better than we ever can.

One study in 2020 found that the average adult will spend the equivalent of 34 years of their lives staring at a screen.[12] In what amounts to over 4,700 hours a year spent looking at phones, laptops and televisions, the people who took part in the survey said they thought less than half the time spent on these devices was 'productive'.

Whilst advances in technology has without question brought a great deal of opportunities, there have been countless studies which show the effect of overuse on our physical and mental health.

> Facebook's motto is 'Screen Time
> not a lifetime.'

7. WE ARE LIVING IN AN 'ALWAYS ON' WORLD

Despite the technology and the progress, ironically in our 24-hour, entertainment-packed modern world, many of us claim to be bored, unstimulated, unamused. I am always reminding my teenage son that I only had four or five TV channels to choose from when I was growing up, and here he is with hundreds, and we still cannot decide on which programme or series to watch.

We are faced with the routine nature of everyday; going to work, food shopping, caring responsibilities and cooking dinner. The monotony of life can be loud and empty at the same time. Despite having the world at our fingertips many would describe being bored or unstimulated. When we are bored, we might find our focus and attention slips and we become apathetic towards life. Whilst boredom is a symptom of some mental health challenges, it can also trigger mental health problems.

We are living in a stimulating, entertaining world which is always available to us, whatever the hour of the day, wherever we are in the world. Maybe we have lost the ability to be bored, to allow our mind to wander freely, to be creative and use our imagination. There is a paradox where everything is available, but we still want more. In a world where we might often say 'that's amazing' maybe we cannot deal with a moment where there is nothing 'amazing' to fill the time.

Children with tablets and devices at the table in restaurants or in shopping trolleys, the growth of in-car entertainment systems and the sight of commuters all looking down at their screens, rather than out of the window, are all evidence of this.

LET'S CHOOSE OUR WORDS CAREFULLY

'As humans, we waste the shit out of our words. It's sad. We use words like "awesome" and "wonderful" like they're candy. It was awesome? Really? It inspired awe? It was wonderful? Are you serious? It was full of wonder? You use the word "amazing" to describe a goddamn sandwich at Wendy's. What's going to happen on your wedding day, or when your first child is born? How will you describe it? You already wasted "amazing" on a fucking sandwich.'

– Louis C.K.

When it comes to finding WOW, you will see that boredom has a starring role to play, and there is a certain amount of reframing to be done on the whole idea of being bored. More on this later.

8. WE ARE LIVING ON AUTOPILOT

In adulthood, with our limited free time, and shortened attention spans we might have the feeling we have 'seen everything before', we have 'been there and done that' and we might not take notice of the details of what's around us.

This 'autopilot' state is all too familiar, maybe you've experienced it yourself on a car journey or commute where you suddenly end up at your destination with no real memory or recollection of how you got there. The wealth of information available on places such as holiday destinations, restaurants and accommodation is so vast we might have the feeling we have 'been' to a place before even travelling there. Reading reviews, looking on Google Earth and watching promotional videos can all diminish the opportunity to discover and experience for ourselves and can put out the fire of WOW before it has even been ignited.

But what if you spend your life on autopilot? Suddenly ending up at your destination, with no real engagement or connection with your journey.

But it's not all bad news, the increased popularity of mindfulness alongside yoga and breathwork is a sign that many of us are reaching out for practices to help combat the modern world. The irony is that a 5,000-year-old practice like meditation, has never been more needed. As we will see, there is no room for the autopilot setting on the road to WOW. So, strap yourself in for a more mindful life.

We might find ourselves asking about life, 'is this it?' but it hasn't always been like this; in childhood we probably wouldn't have asked this existential question. Most of us can remember times we were immersed, surprised, amazed, fascinated by the expanding world around us. The future was a blank canvas, likely full of hope and ambition. It is time to rekindle this fire, the mindset, this spirit, this attitude to life.

Growing up in West Somerset, I was surrounded by national parks, a seemingly endless coastline and rolling hills. Every Sunday afternoon walk was filled with natural treasures, expanding views and WOW. Looking for fossils in the rocks, picking blackberries to make jam or climbing cliffs from the beach hunting for treasures in a redundant Victorian rubbish tip, there was a WOW every single time.

We are living in a world which has wonder all around us. We know this. We saw this and articulated this as a child. We are just not so easily open to WOW anymore. But the good news is, this can change.

Find Your WOW helps you learn to rediscover small moments of awe in the everyday, many of which are totally free and might just be the key to our health and happiness.

'Mystery creates wonder and wonder is the basis of Man's desire to understand.'

– Neil Armstrong

Chapter 3.

The science of WOW

If we say, albeit with a little tongue in cheek, that we are living in a WOW-less world, it is important to consider what the consequences might be, of living without WOW. Why do we need it, and what happens if we lack WOW in our life?

The closest scientists have come to studying the experience of WOW, is the increasingly popular area of research surrounding the feeling of awe. In the past decade, academics and psychologists have rapidly started to study the effect of 'awe', or the lack of awe experiences on our physical and mental health and well-being.

In modern research, awe is defined as an emotional experience where we are 'so overwhelmed by the vastness or greatness of something to the point it alters how we view or understand the world.'[1]

Barbara Fredrickson in her book Positivity wrote[2]: 'Awe happens when you come across goodness on a grand scale. You literally feel overwhelmed by greatness. By comparison, you feel small and humble. Awe makes you stop in your tracks. You are momentarily transfixed. Boundaries melt away and you feel part of something larger than yourself.

Mentally, you're challenged to absorb and accommodate the sheer scale of what you've encountered. Awe, like gratitude and inspiration, is a self-transcendent emotion.'

In one landmark study,[3] psychologists Dacher Keltner and Jonathan Haidt discovered that there are two criteria that determine whether something is truly an awe experience: '**perceived vastness**' and a '**need for accommodation**'.

'**Perceived vastness**' might come from observing something physically large such as the Grand Canyon, but also from a theoretical sense of vastness, such as witnessing someone with a great talent.

An experience evokes a '**need for accommodation**' when it exceeds our expectations in some way or changes our understanding of the world.

According to science, when we experience awe, it is often accompanied by feelings of self-diminishment (where we feel small) and increased connectedness with other people. Interestingly, the researchers found that experiencing awe can even take people into a self-transcendent state, where they focus less on themselves and feel more like a part of something bigger, so awe is thought of as changing our consciousness as well as being a pure emotional state.

As children, we are literally small, and life opens up for us a little more day by day. We learn more about the world and ourselves, and from moment to moment we change our opinion and perception on things. Our minds are a sponge for knowledge. We are in a school system, set up with the intention to help us learn, grow and thrive. We are ripe for awe experiences. We accept we are little, and we view the world with awe and wonder because, although we might not realise that at the time, this is our purpose.

The studies into the science of awe and wonder may be the closest researchers have got to (scientifically) describing what it feels like to experience what I call WOW.

What are the other health benefits of awe? How can encountering, experiencing and engineering more awe in your everyday life affect your body and mind?

Experiencing awe can reduce stress levels within the body. In one study, researchers examined the effect of an awe experience (a day's river rafting trip), on city-dwelling high school students and war veterans. All participants said time spent outdoors and being in nature induced a sense of awe that led to reduced levels of stress, an improvement in their overall well-being and a reduction in their symptoms of PTSD, which were lowered for weeks after the trip itself.[4]

One of the researchers said: '[The evidence supporting the link between spending time outdoors, experiencing awe and lower stress levels] has become so persuasive that medical professionals have begun to "prescribe" time spent in nature or in green spaces, the way one might typically prescribe a new medication.'

Experiencing awe can expand our sense of time, can help us cope with uncertainty and make us less prone to impatience. At some point in your life, you will have experienced waiting for news of some kind. Whether it is the results of an exam, a job interview or medical tests.

Scientists have found that experiencing a feeling of awe, may be the best way to alleviate the discomfort that comes from uncertain waiting.

One researcher, Kate Sweeny[5] explored the most excruciating form of waiting, which is the period of awaiting uncertain news, the outcome of which is beyond your control. Her research found ways to alleviate those difficult periods included meditation, engaging in 'flow' activities, and experiences that require complete focus, such as playing a video game. Time spent in nature also helped, and even watching an awe-inspiring video, although she adds 'meditation is not for everyone, and it can be difficult to achieve a state of flow when worry is raging out of control.'

The concept of awe has only recently received attention in psychology, but 'now that we know we can make people feel better through brief awe experiences while they're waiting, we can take this knowledge out into the real world to see if people feel less stressed when they watch "Planet Earth" or go to an observatory, for example, while they're suffering through a difficult waiting period.'

It might be that by experiencing awe we are changing our perception of time and furthermore, how we feel time. When we experience awe, time expands, and our normal 'mundane concerns' fade.[6] This sense of timelessness makes us feel more patient. There is a clear connection between awe, WOW and the state of flow, which we will examine in later chapters.

Encountering awe can make us kinder One study[7] asked students to spend a minute either staring at a beautiful eucalyptus tree on campus, or a 'drab' science block building. When a 'stranger' walked by and 'accidentally' dropped a box of pens, those participants who had gazed at the trees were more likely to help the stranger collect the pens. Researchers found that when we have more awe-inducing experiences or encounter more awe and wonder, our sense of community grows stronger, and we have a greater sense of 'collective' over individual needs.[8] By enabling us to feel connected to each other, form alliances, act generously and explore new possibilities.[9] Summer Allen writes in a White Paper about the mysterious and complex emotion known as 'awe':[10] 'Awe experiences are self-transcendent. They shift our attention away from ourselves, make us feel like we are part of something greater than ourselves, and make us more generous towards others.'[11]

Awe experiences can possibly help alleviate symptoms of pain. One pain specialist, Michael Amster, researched the effects of awe on people suffering from chronic pain. Experiencing moments of awe did far more than he expected: 'Many of them reported a significant decrease in chronic pain, this was pain that I was never able to help with medications, injections, or surgery.'

What does it feel like to experience awe? What are the symptoms of awe? If you encounter something awe-inspiring, you might have experienced some of the following symptoms; maybe there's a jaw drop, a sharp intake of breath, tears, feeling of euphoria, your heart seemingly skips a beat.

Allen describes the symptoms of experiencing awe

as physical changes in the body such as spine tingles, goosebumps, shivers, chills or a release of energy. You may feel more alert and take deeper breaths, your facial expression may change, with a smile, wide eyes, raised eyebrows and a relaxed jaw.

These are all automatic reactions, and most cannot be faked. I am sure you know how it feels when you encounter awe and wonder, and it is likely that it is not those two words which come from your mouth, it is much more likely that you say one word. WOW.

What is your prescription, how much awe do we need in our life? How much of a difference would a monthly, weekly or daily dose of awe make to our well-being? One study[12] found that participants who experienced awe twice a week on average led to them having greater well-being and life satisfaction up to three weeks later. The lasting effect of awe on our health and happiness seems substantial. Experiencing awe a few times a day, maybe for just 30 seconds each time could start to make a real difference.

But is awe just available to the spiritual and the enlightened? Jake Eagle, a therapist who lives in Hawaii said: 'Awe is available to all of us, and it's available most of the time.'

Research shows that **we do not even need to experience awe in the real world**. Simply **seeing images or video of awe-inspiring scenes** can invoke the same health and well-being benefits. In one study when participants were shown a slideshow of either common place nature scenes (for example, an oak tree), or an awe-inspiring nature scene of say, the Grand Canyon, both groups showed an increase in positive mood, but those who watched the latter 'awe' slideshow reported a far greater improvement.[13]

When we experience awe, we feel small, and our attention shifts to the wider world rather than ourselves — and past work on adults has suggested that this fosters prosocial behaviour that benefits others.

A new study has found that feelings of awe also make children more prosocial too. This is perhaps unsurprising, as the authors of the new paper in Psychological Science wrote: 'Intrinsically curious and hungry for the mysterious, children are built for awe.'[14]

At the time of writing, the Aurora Borealis, or Northern Lights, have been visible in the night sky to many parts of the UK, with wonderful awe-inspiring pictures being shared by the media, on social media and WhatsApp groups all over the country and one word has been heard the most, WOW. So it seems awe not only makes us feel good, perhaps even healthier in our body and mind, it might also improve our relationships and help us feel more connected to others or a part of something bigger. And that's got to be a good thing, right?

So, are you ready to Find Your WOW?

'Be absolutely assured that we will die long before our own deaths if we ever allow the fear of adulthood to kill the wonder of childhood.'

– Craig D Lounsbrough

Chapter 4.

The 15 reasons children find meditation easier than adults

So far, we have considered the world we are living in, looked at some of the research which is the closest we can get to WOW, the study of awe. Now I want to take you right back to where I began, talking about what children have, and what we have lost in adulthood (what I am calling WOW), and how we might be able to get this back.

This book was inspired by a question I was asked repeatedly when teaching mindfulness in businesses and organisations, when executives found out that I also taught meditation to children in schools, 'Wow! How do you teach a four-year-old to meditate?'

At first, I didn't know the answer, I thought 'maybe it is to do with them being at school, and learning all the time...' Because children are used to being told what to do and discipline and routine is a part of their life. To some, I was just another teacher at their school teaching them something they didn't yet know how to do. But after a while, I began to consider it might be more than this.

After I had been asked the question for what seemed like the millionth time, I began to make a note of my observations from teaching children to try and reflect on why it might be that 'children, learn mindfulness far easier, than say, a 54-year-old.'

But these 15 reasons were not enough on their own, surely there was a simpler and bigger explanation. What skill or gift do children HAVE, that we LOSE as adults, and could this be the secret to unlocking why they are so often natural meditators?

Soon, from my observations of teaching meditation to over 15,000 children, I had formed 15 reasons why children are much better at practising mindfulness than adults. From this, I went on a journey of research, discovery and reflection. This period just so happened to be during a global pandemic, when I continued to teach mindfulness to children and adults, albeit online. By this point, I was also teaching mindfulness at a leading business school. I realised I was in an unrivalled position to compare the experience of teaching mindfulness to both five-year-olds (just embarking on their educational journey), at the same time as teaching very experienced (and often academically gifted), individuals who have gained a senior position in their career. I was now sensemaking my observations into something more concrete.

The truth is (and we would probably never tell them this), how you teach a four-year-old primary school pupil, and a 54-year-old is the same. You keep it simple, you start small and leave out anything spiritual. But what is often the obvious difference from the outset, is the attitude or the mindset towards learning something new.

What follows are my 15 observations on why children are more natural meditators than adults, but I need to explain their connection to Find Your WOW. Afterall, that's why you're here.

Each of the 15 observations are incredibly useful standalone life lessons. But once pulled together, they help us unlock the secret of why children still have WOW in their life, and we have lost ours. You might like to take these life lessons on board as if a child-age version of you is reading them.

The 15 observations are the building blocks and foundation of the WOW framework. Before we embark on a journey to Find Your WOW, to rediscover a childlike awe and wonder of life, and look at the world with new eyes (which might just save your mind), let's take a moment to ponder on those 15 observations, because even if you stop reading the book here, I think you might find them useful.

THE 15 REASONS WHY CHILDREN FIND MEDITATION EASIER THAN ADULTS

1. Children are naturally mindful, live in the here and now, and do not find multitasking easy

Children live in the here and now; if you have ever asked a young child what they did at school earlier that day, they might not be able to tell you. We might think this is lazy or rude, but the fact is – a lot has happened since then. Whilst this might be frustrating for adults, for children they are generally able to easily move on from experiments, incidents and accidents that happen throughout their day. Children often do not carry baggage from one day to the next. This is why when they fall out with friends and are devastated one moment, you might turn around and see them playing together again in the next, or perhaps hanging out with a completely new set of friends within a heartbeat.

Of course, there are traumatic events, which affect children to the core, and I am writing this with a broad-brush approach, talking about most children and how they approach their daily life, but sadly there will always be exceptions.

When my son was around three or four years old, he loved to play with his little Matchbox toy cars, using the grooves in our wooden floorboards as roads. He would lie on his belly, completely immersed in the scene, his eyeline at the steering wheel of the car, making the sounds of the engine, driving perfectly on the tiny kitchen floor motorway. The little wheels of the car would perfectly find their groove in the wooden grains, and if ever I called his name, he would rarely respond, so immersed was he in his game. Was he being defiant or ignoring me? Or was he so in the state of flow that his play was a meditation in itself?

If you have any experience of children, you will know that this is their way. They do one thing at a time and cannot, or will not, attempt more. They are residing in the present. As we will discover, it is biology that is behind this mindful living. The natural brainwave state of a child under eight years old is in fact the same brainwave state we reach when we practise mindfulness meditation.

Children are masters of mindfulness because they are literally made that way. As we grow older and move towards the brainwave state of an adult, we start to try and multitask, become more easily distracted and are not so able to immerse ourselves in activities.

Children's brains develop quickly, but they find it difficult, if not impossible, to try and do more than one thing at a time. You may have witnessed the complete concentration of a young child painting a picture, tongue hanging out, living and breathing that masterpiece. When confronted with a blank page, they just get started, but having attended my own occasional art class in adulthood, the same cannot be said about grown-ups.

Children also do not bring up past experiences and memories to the current situation and don't think too much about what lies ahead. What is important is the here and now, and no more (see next point).

Lesson to learn: Try and be in the present, the here and now, just focus on one thing, don't try and multitask. Everything else can wait.

2. Children have a natural slow pace of life, little sense of time or concept of past and future

The words 'slow' and 'children' might not always seem to go hand in hand, as you watch them race around the playground, park or living room. It might be more accurate to say that children go at their own pace; when they want to run and play, they run, when they want to take 45 minutes choosing their outfit for a party, they will, when they want to stop and examine every crack in the pavement to look for bugs, they do.

Children really don't like to be rushed. They have their own natural rhythm which, at times, is not quite the same rhythm as grown-ups who have a bit of a tight schedule. Whether it is to get out of the door for school, or to make an appointment or to get to the party on time. I will talk more about this in later chapters and how adults are guilty of speeding up the pace of life for children. To a certain extent it needs to be this way, otherwise nothing would ever get done and none of us would never get anywhere 'on time'. But sometimes, and I hold my hands up to this, we can be guilty of being busy or fast-paced for no reason.

We are rushing and we don't even know why.

As adults and parents, we are the gatekeepers of time. We are preoccupied, maybe even obsessed with it. We are constantly clock watching to see when we need to race out the door to the next activity; assessing windows of time to squeeze in another load of washing and preparing dinner while checking emails or having a conversation and so on and so on.

Winnie-the-Pooh and Piglet summarised this concept very well:

'What day is it?' asked Pooh. 'It's today,' squeaked Piglet.
'My favourite day,' said Pooh.'

– **AA Milne**

Children do not have a fully developed sense of time, including history and future, until they are around eight years old. Before that, they are at the mercy of adults to help them. As we will see in the coming chapters, this age of our development, also coincides with being the prime time to experience WOW; when children are exploring, learning, in awe and wonder of the world around them and suddenly, the adults around them are wondering what time it is, and whether they can make it to the supermarket before it closes.

Swiss psychologist, Jean Piaget[1] researched how children relate to 'time'. (My partner is Swiss, and I often tease him about his incredulous punctuality and the efficiency of his beautiful country, so you can imagine how happy he was when I discovered this fact.) Piaget discovered that at around seven or eight years old, children start to think logically and begin to solve more complex problems, but before this age young children are unable to evaluate time. At eight years old, although children are able to count time, they do not spontaneously think of doing so unless instructed to by an adult.

Time is one thing, but when do we begin to have a sense

of past and future? The study of 'future thinking' is being increasingly researched within psychology. The idea of mentally projecting yourself forward in time is thought to be uniquely human and studies suggest this ability is starting to be in place by ages four or five years old.[2] In a study that looked at whether children and adults would report past or future thoughts; only adults showed a future-oriented bias and more than a third of the youngest age group in the study (six to seven years) produced no thoughts of future events at all.[3]

Children are experts of being right here, right now.

Conversation between me and my son when he was around four or five years old:

'What did you have for lunch at school today?'

'I can't remember, Mummy.'

'Can you try and think, as I don't want to cook the same thing as you already had.'

'But I don't mind having the same thing again. I like the same.'

Lesson to learn: Slow down, don't rush, try not to think about the past or the future and don't worry about what the time is.

3. Children often show unconditional love towards others
I remember it so clearly, I had just finished teaching a yoga class of around 30 seven- and eight-year-old children, we had said goodbye and thank you to each other and I started to roll up the yoga mats when suddenly I felt an impact, a pair of arms wrapped around my waist. 'Thankkkk youuuuu,' came the little voice as one girl hugged me, and then… it was a

hug tsunami. One after one, five or six children came up and hugged me, sometimes hugging the child who was already attached to me, sometimes waiting patiently for their hug moment. I had previously worked in the corporate world, so this was a whole new experience for me, to be hugged after a piece of work. And it brought a tear to my eye.

This started to become a common occurrence. Sometimes when just walking through a school corridor, a child who had remembered me from a previous visit would hail 'Looooossseeeee' and I would wait for the impact of the hug. Children often say, and show, how they feel without limitation, and this is a beautiful thing. They show love unconditionally and show their love through little gestures and sometimes, not so little hugs.

Lesson to learn: Love.

4. Children are in a daily environment of learning, being challenged and receiving feedback, and they are used to (and often not afraid of) making mistakes (aka the red pen)

When a child is at school, one of their main jobs each day, is to learn. Correction, when a child is at school one of their main jobs each day, is to make mistakes and to learn. Aside from all the other physical and emotional development going on inside them at this time, which is vast and not to be overlooked, learning is their big job.

Most of a child's daily life between the age of 4 and 16 years old is spent in a learning environment, with teachers who teach, and with time to be creative, play and experiment.

Minute by minute they are discovering new things which broaden their horizons, change perspectives and open up the world for them just a little bit more.

And of course, when this amount of learning is going on, mistakes will be made. Little red ticks will be added up to tot up scores, little crosses will indicate that they didn't get something right. And the sheer amount of feedback and scoring and assessing means that a child is used to making mistakes.

**Getting things wrong is a key part of learning.
Mistakes are a key part of life.**

You won't get in very much trouble for the mistakes you make as an eight-year-old, especially if you tried your best. So, if therefore, you don't grasp something first time, this is normal, this is life. You can't afford to give up after falling at the first hurdle, there's no time for this, you have other stuff to get on with. Every hour of every school day is spent learning something new, being challenged, and you are growing.

When someone throws another skill into the learning mix like mindfulness meditation, you simply face this with the same mindset you face all the other skills you are trying to get to grips with; algebra, spelling, balancing in gym class. Mindfulness? No problem.

Lesson to learn: Don't worry about making mistakes, fail fast and learn quickly, move on, don't fear the red pen.

5. Children can access the state of flow easily

You will read later in the book that the natural brainwave state of children, up to the age of around eight, is Alpha and this is the brainwave state we might access when we practise mindfulness. Moreover, up until the age of six they are naturally in the brainwave state of Theta, which are the brainwaves we access in the flow state, and this is why they are able to focus and completely absorb themselves in a task. The flow state is where there is a balance of challenge and skill level, and you are just on the edge of your ability, on the verge of something being too difficult.

Children in an environment of learning and gradual progression through a specifically designed curriculum, with teachers to support them, are naturally pushed to get to the next level and also access the state of flow regularly throughout the day. In many schools, children are encouraged to develop a growth mindset and taught to be motivated by the process, not the goal itself. A growth mindset helps children to cope with difficult things and grow the belief that they'll be fine, despite challenge.

People who frequently find access to the flow state are called autotelic personalities, which means they are motivated by the process rather than what might be the reward or achievement at the end.

These personalities tend to have a sense of curiosity and urge to discover new things whilst staying persistent, focussed and committed with narrow-minded focus, secondly, to be self-confident, whilst losing a sense of self, and to show independence but able to cooperate with others. Which sounds like a lot of children I know. You could argue that in childhood, most children are naturally autotelic.

This is backed up by research in which three groups of children were asked to play sports, with varying levels of reward; one group was extrinsically motivated by the chance of receiving a 'good player award', one group received an unexpected award, and thirdly a group who received no reward. In the free play period, those who did not expect any award played for a longer amount of time, with the conclusion that extrinsic motivation affects intrinsic motivation.[4]

Finding access to the flow state in adulthood is thought to help us become up to five times more productive, reduce chances of burnout, make us feel more relaxed and at ease and is the gateway to effortless peak performance. Not only that, but it also increases creativity, improves a sense of happiness, and greater sense of meaning and improves our overall health and well-being. All from getting yourself into the zone.

As you will learn in later chapters, when we are in flow (because of a down regulation of a part of the brain called the Prefrontal Cortex) our sense of time and perspective is altered, our stress levels are lowered, we forget distractions, and can even forget what we need such as hunger, thirst and other thoughts.

TEN WAYS TO HELP CHILDREN (OR YOURSELF) FIND FLOW:

- Find or explore activities which give room for self-exploration. What do you already enjoy doing which encourages self-expression or self-development?
- Be part of a group. Research shows that singing in choirs or taking part in other 'group flow' activities not only reduces stress but also increases the ability to access flow on an individual level.
- Let frustration be part of the game and learn how to deal with it. Not only does frustration improve emotional resilience and well-being, when you make mistakes and FAIL, you are growing the part of the brain which builds self-belief, self-confidence and motivation. Accessing the flow state is about finding the balance between ideal challenge and ideal skill, but the key thing to remember is you are measuring a perception of what you are capable of. So as long as you are (or your child is) not overwhelmed, by pushing yourself to the edge of your comfort zone you are improving your self-efficacy, building the growth mindset and are more likely to accept new challenges going forward, all of which becomes a self-fulfilling cycle.
- Choose what you spotlight your focus on, limit distractions.
- Make it FUN, focus on positive, have a playful attitude.
- Explore emotions and increase self-awareness of how you feel.

- Build on your strengths, create your flow strategy which can be used in all areas of your life including work, parenting and relationships.
- Visualise the process.
- Adapt goals.
- Increase intrinsic motivation and interest.

Lesson to learn: Get in the zone, go with the flow, let yourself become immersed in what you are doing, forget everything else, it can wait.

6. Children have unrestrained creativity and playfulness, and their purpose is to learn and play

As Albert Einstein once said: 'To stimulate creativity, one must develop the childlike inclination for play.'

So, what exactly is the link between childhood and creativity? Why are children so creative and so good at playing, and maybe, how can we generate more of this creative energy in adulthood?

I once asked a class of seven-year-olds for as many uses as they could think of for a clothes peg. As you might imagine, I got a washing line full of brilliant, clever, innovative and often hilariously funny, answers. Children are divergent thinkers which means they can produce a whole range of ideas, freely and enthusiastically without – crucially, as we will see in later chapters – an inner critic having a quiet word in their ear. The same of which cannot be said about us adults.

Why is this? One key part of the brain that is still in

development when we are children is the frontal cortex which (amongst other things) is responsible for cognitive skills such as problem solving, language and other important functions. It is not until we are in our early 20s that the frontal cortex becomes more 'rational' which means we are able to make informed judgements and decisions. One downside though, is that we start to lose our ability for divergent thinking which can kill our creativity and ability to play more freely. See also my 4th observation that children are used to making mistakes, and as adults we tend to view a mistake as a failure, instead of a natural and healthy part of the creation process and you can see it's a recipe for creative disaster.

On the contrary, messing up is an important and natural part of the creative process. Author and artist Charlie Mackesy[5] who wrote the bestselling The Boy, the Mole, the Fox and the Horse, which is one my favourite books to turn to when I am in need of an immediate moment of WOW, said (when interviewed for a TV documentary surrounded by a pile of his sketches, thousands of which did not even make it into the book): 'We are surrounded by a sea of errors, if you keep going, you might just find something worth keeping.' This illustrates the creative process and how important it is to experiment, learn and persist. Watch any child at play, and you'll see this is true. And maybe the more you allow yourself to make mistakes, the more likely you are to innovate and find something new.

FIVE WAYS YOU CAN STIMULATE YOUR CREATIVE
BRAIN AND RECAPTURE YOUR CHILDLIKE CREATIVITY:

- **Take a play break:** Throughout the day, stop what you are doing to listen to music, play with a toy or doodle on a piece of paper. Stretching your brain in different ways and daydreaming can stimulate your imagination. **Challenge:** How many things can you make with a pile of paper clips?

- **Allow yourself to mess up:** Making mistakes can open doors to new possibilities and solutions. **Challenge:** Wear something you wouldn't normally be caught dead in and pay attention to the feelings and sensations that arise. Notice that these feelings are fleeting.

- **Move your body:** Regular physical movement can help stimulate your hippocampus,[6] which some researchers believe can enhance your imaginative abilities. **Challenge:** Go to the park and fly a kite, play frisbee or have a go on a rope swing.

- **Be more like a kid:** Play, try new things and make mistakes. Wear something weird. Daydream and look at the clouds. Make your own rules, exploring new ideas, and most of all — play. **Challenge:** Do something for no purpose other than play or creativity itself, break the rules.

- **See things from a different perspective:** Try to see a situation, problem or experience from a different viewpoint to your usual one. For example, through the eyes of a child, from a person with a disability or someone from a different culture. **Challenge:** Explore Edward de Bono's concept of

'Six Thinking Hats',[7] which is a way of looking at an issue from a variety of perspectives. The technique encourages you to consider a problem in six different ways, with no right or wrong answer. Each of the 'Thinking Hats' represent a different option, viewpoint or perspective. For example, the 'Green Hat' represents creative thinking, when you wear this hat, you look at a range of ideas and possible ways forward, the 'Red Hat' is for the heart (feelings and instincts) and the 'Yellow Hat' is the Optimists' hat where you look at issues with a positive light.

Lesson to learn: Rediscover the child within.

7. Children are often happy with small, simple things

Because everything is new when you are a child, it often does not matter whether that new thing costs nothing or several hundred pounds. If you have been around children on Christmas morning, you will probably have seen the delight the little ones take from playing with the box the toy has come in, rather than the toy itself.

As we know, children love to live in an imaginary world full of make-believe and creativity. In that empty cardboard box, you have given them the greatest gift, a blank canvas of possibility which can be literally anything in the world they choose. Children are only limited by what their imaginations can come up with. The cardboard box plays such an essential part of childhood play that in 2005 it was even put into the USA National Toy Hall of Fame.

Whereas an adult sees a cardboard box as something to be broken down for the recycling, if children are faced with one, they love to take over control of it, to own it, which prompts them to be creative. When children express themselves, they can experiment, try new ideas, problem solve and more. Imagination is important in child development because a key set of personal, social and physical skills are learned in the process of being imaginative.

When your brain imagines being part of an activity, the brain is activated in the same way as it would be if the activity was being completed. Therefore, when a child is playing with a cardboard box, perhaps pretending they are driving a car, they really can be taken to anywhere to do anything at all they choose. There is a world of other benefits including concentration, focus, entertainment and feeling secure in their own space. In this unstructured play, they use a wide range of social, negotiation and problem-solving skills to act out stories, this might involve putting themselves in the shoes of another person, which increases empathic development.

Lesson to learn: Be creative just for the sake of it, and make more time to play.

8. Children will often say no to the things they do not want to do, they 'know their own mind'

Children will often say no to the things they do not want to do, and this is certainly particularly true of the pre-schooler and toddler children who are sometimes portrayed as demanding or selfish 'in the terrible twos.' But on the contrary, the 'saying-no-to-everything' stage is a crucial part of the child's brain development and demonstrates strong control and boundaries which are being set by the child.

Kathryn Smerling,[8] a New York Family Psychologist explains: 'Children are experiencing the most rapid brain development of their life. Around the age of 3, can you believe as many as 700 brand new neural connections are formed every SINGLE SECOND. By the end of this developmental explosion in toddlerhood is the "no phase".'

In this phase, children are learning valuable life lessons about relationships, consent, self-care and their limitations. They are acting from their truest self, unmoulded by social conformities, gaining independence and experiencing so many crucial developments.

Lesson to learn: Life is too short to say yes to things you don't want to do, listen to your heart and say no.

9. They have an underdeveloped sense of the self, a lack of ego and little comparison to others

This point is fundamental, and I have devoted a whole chapter to it later in the book, but what we will learn is that in childhood up until the age of around eight, children have an underdeveloped sense of self, ego and are only just beginning to understand and comprehend their place in the world. But a LOT more on this later.

This is illustrated most starkly by the number of hands

which go up in class in response to a question I might ask. If I ask a question in school years 1–4, (from age five up until around nine years old) hands will shoot up, lots of them, with enthusiastic faces looking to share and take part. Ask a question in school years 5 or 6 (children aged nine to eleven) you might get a few hands, and it will normally be the same faces who offer to contribute.

The self-awareness, the self-consciousness and a sense of self is starting to creep in. They might be concerned how they will look and be perceived not just by me as their teacher, but perhaps more importantly by their fellow classmates. The children are beginning to get a sense of their place in the world and a sense of a pecking order in their class community.

Lesson to learn: Remember who you really are, you are unique, don't compare yourself to others and don't worry about what others think.

10. There are no limitations to their hopes, dreams and ambitions

This point is linked to the previous one of a lack of self, if you ask any young child what job they might like to have when they are older, their answer will be driven by their deepest dreams and ideas, drawn from books they have been read or films they have watched and been inspired by.

It's universally cute when little children announce that when they grow up they intend to become astronauts, pop stars or the Prime Minister.[9] My friend, who lives in New York, once sent me a photograph of her six-year-old twin daughters, one is dressed as a princess AND is wearing a police badge, because... when she is older, she wants to be a princess AND a police officer. And who am I to argue?

Until a child reaches late childhood, their hopes and dreams and ambitions are limitless, anything is possible.

As parents and adults, it might be tempting to temper a child's dreams sooner rather than later, but some interesting research suggests in fact we should encourage children to dream big and aim high. One recently published study[10] analysed surveys of 17,000 children conducted 10 times from 1958 for over 60 years, it found that when it comes to how much children achieve in life, big dreams matter as much if not more than IQ or the family's socio-economic situation.[11]

The study revealed that while socio-economic circumstances influenced a child's future goals, the reverse is also true, and adults have a big role in shaping those dreams. Research 'found that parents' desires for their children's future were a stronger influence on their aspirations and, eventually, their achievements, than their socioeconomic background.'[12] The higher children aimed in life, the more successful they became. And the audaciousness of the children's dreams had a lot to do with how much their parents and teachers encouraged them to dream.

And interestingly, the size of kids' dreams mattered even

more for girls than boys, the takeaway for parents (and teachers) is that encouraging kids to dream big despite the limitations of their current circumstances really, really matters. 'Inequality begins early on, with a child's aspirations. Parental aspirations concerning their children's school and career performance have a particularly great effect on how far a child aims to go.'[13]

Lesson to learn: Dream big, anything is possible.

11. Children are in touch with their emotions

Go to any classroom, in any school in the UK (and probably Europe and US), and you are likely to see some form of emotions wallchart. Children are encouraged to track how they are feeling each day, with colours and stickers with smiley faces, to help them to become more aware of situations which affect their emotions and how they are feeling. There's a great adult version of this by the way, in app form, called MOOD, established by Welsh developer, Gareth Dauncey.

In childhood, our 'learning and rational' brain is still developing, our neocortex doesn't finish wiring up until we are about 25 years old. However, our limbic system, which is responsible for our emotions, is already fully working in childhood. This means a child's emotions are much more accessible than their reason, so they will talk and act with their heart over their head.

As we grow older, we learn more rational ways to temper and cope with our emotions, as our neocortex matures. This is a crucial part of a child's brain and social development, and helping them to understand, identify and cope with their emotions is crucial, and needs to be supported and encouraged.

Increasing awareness of our emotions is an important step on the road to developing emotional intelligence and becoming an adult human. As children become more familiar with a full vocabulary of emotional language, they become better at pinpointing what they are experiencing. Emotional connection and regulation are essential building blocks of life.

Lesson to learn: How are you? I mean, how are you really? Listen to your emotions.

12. **Children have a natural state of awe and wonder, and they are not afraid of asking questions or being inquisitive**

But why, but why, but why? Maybe you have experienced this line of questioning in your time, the like of which would make a high court barrister envious. But this has not come from the mouth of an educated man or woman of the chambers, this is coming from the four-year-old standing in front of you.

Children are naturally curious, of course they are, their whole world is starting to pop and open around them. Asking questions is an important – essential – part of understanding and in making sense of what is happening. More than that, a child's curiosity helps them to develop skills, vocabulary and concepts.

'Curiosity is one of the permanent and certain characteristics of a vigorous intellect.'

– Samuel Johnson

According to a recent article in the Independent,[14] curious children ask on average 73 questions per day. This in turn, might lead parents to go on Google 73 more times than they would have done otherwise. But it is around the age of four, just as many children start school, that the curiosity bug is at its height, and the resulting effect is that children shower questions day and night to anyone who will listen.

As children grow up it's natural for them to be curious about the world. As parents it's easy to forget just how much of our children's knowledge comes from what we tell them. Questions are extremely important for childhood development and a child's first experiences in asking and answering 'why' questions in their quest to understand the world they live in are the building blocks of deep thinking and will help prepare them for the future.

Children are in awe and wonder of the world, and when they are in full flow, you are most likely to hear the word WOW from a child. When you reveal that octopuses really have three hearts, that humans can hold our breath for two to three minutes (no Johnny, please don't try that now) and a full cumulus cloud can weigh the same as full packed passenger jet. The response is almost always WOW, and this is a regular occurrence, because everything is new, everything is wonderous and almost everything is WOW.

Whether they are asking out loud, whispering questions to their best friend sitting in the next chair or questioning themselves in their head, you can be sure that a child is pretty much always, asking questions. And my goodness, they like to ask questions.

Lesson to learn: Never stop asking why, always ask questions, never stop wondering, never stop learning.

13. Children have an inherent connection to, and are easily enthralled by nature

Nature is often one of a young child's main sources of curiosity, inspiration and entertainment. Watching birds or insects, building bug hotels, playing in streams, watching cloud patterns, playing on the beach; there is so much to learn. All whilst often getting their hands (and every other part of their body) dirty.

Within a generation, however, children's lives have largely moved indoors, and with it a loss of the free-range exploration of the nearby natural world. In 2015, wildlife conservation charity, the RSPB found that older children who are spending more time on screens, are losing their connection with nature and this could have damaging consequences for them and the planet.[15]

Children are innate scientists and love to experiment and experience the sights, scents, sounds and textures of the outdoors. Nature provides countless opportunities for discovery, creativity, problem-solving and other learning. Children's feelings of empathy are also enhanced through contact with nature, and they learn to care more about the well-being of other living things.

Time spent in nature, even for just a short time, has been shown to restore children's cognitive abilities, improve attention spans and boost mental resilience. Studies even showed this to be the case when just a view of nature was available from the classroom.[16]

When we are exposed to a natural environment, stress is reduced on both a mental and physiological level. In studies, stress hormones and blood pressure levels both improved after spending time in nature, helping children both physically and emotionally. Research has found so many benefits for children from being in nature (and many of them go for adults too). The opportunity to exercise, the experience of a better quality of sleep after spending time out in nature, improved social skills and the possibility to discover new skills like leadership, problem-solving, teamwork and even risk-assessment.[17]

Children can feel a part of something bigger by understanding the vastness of the planet, that's why so many enjoy watching nature programmes where they can learn and be inspired and feel connected to their ever-expanding world.

Lesson to learn: Never take the natural world for granted, look after it, love it, learn and be curious about it, treasure it, protect it.

14. Children often have a default state of positivity and happiness

Happiness is just one of the wide range of feelings and emotions we will feel at different points and stages of our life. We are not supposed to be happy all the time, but to have an overall sense of happiness and well-being is what many of us are striving for.

Happiness is of course subjective and whatever our age, we will still face difficult times. But in general, children are happier and have lower overall stress levels than adults, and as we will see in the coming chapters, there has been a wealth of research which shows our happiness peaks in childhood, tends to dip during adolescence all the way down to middle age, where it is at its lowest, and then begins to rise again to another high point of happiness in our old age.

An average day at school for a child, although structured with learning, will also include fun activities, social and playtime with friends (often outside in the fresh air), opportunities to be creative and time to do some exercise. These are all important pieces of the jigsaw for our physical and mental health and well-being and to feeling happier.

It is important to note, there are also a significant number of children who are working through mental health challenges (statistics range from 1 in 3 to 1 in 4 children with a diagnosed condition). There will be experts who will disagree with this, but there have been many studies which show that childhood is amongst the happiest years of your life. This is linked to the fact that children are very often happy with small things, and do not yet have the pressure to conform and have the level of responsibilities felt in adulthood. It is thought that up to half of our happiness is genetically predetermined, but linked to my earlier observation, children can be in touch with their emotions and to a certain extent, their minds are free.

Lesson to learn: You don't always have to be happy, but learn what brings you happiness and try to do that more often.

15. Children do not feel guilty about taking time to do things for themselves

Children need lots of things to be done for them; caring, teaching and the logistics or heavy lifting of life are done by other people around them, their parents and carers and teachers. Linked to my earlier point of not being afraid to say no, children's brains are not fully developed for rational thinking, and they are led by their heart.

As we grow older, there are likely to be fewer people around us to take care and do things for us, so the onus is on us and that is an essential part of being an adult, and developing an emotional intelligence is taking care and responsibility for our own health and well-being.

Lesson to learn: Try not to feel guilty about doing things for yourself, from making time for hobbies to self-care and development. Make time to do the things you need, want and love to do.

'As parents we should give our children two things; roots and wings.'

– Goethe

I would like to thank all the 15,000 primary school children who I was lucky enough to spend time with from 2016 to 2023 and thank you for inspiring me every day. These original 15 observations started my journey to discover what we have an abundance of as children and have lost in adulthood and crucially work out how we might be able to get it back. These 15 observations, as we will now go on to read, are the basis for the foundations for the WOW framework, which will hopefully help you to Find Your WOW.

- By slowing down time (Being in the **NOW**)
- Increasing your **FOCUS** and letting go of distractions
- Accessing the state of **FLOW**
- Letting go of **EGO** and the inner critic or voice
- To then cultivate the conditions for **WOW**

'To grow up is to wonder about things; to be grown up is to slowly forget the things you wondered about as a child.'

– Henning Mankell

Chapter 5.

Why children are the masters of WOW

In my opening chapters I declared that children are naturally mindful and my experience of teaching thousands of adults and children in parallel showed me that they find the ancient practice of meditation much easier than their grown-up counterparts. Since forming my 15 observations, from the last chapter, I have spent the past few years digging into research and studies into the deeper reason why this might be.

In childhood, the whole wide world is 'opening up' tiny moment by tiny moment, each day filled with a journey of exploration and discovery. Children have so much to learn, and their brains can only process the immediate, in its full technicoloured wonder, often not tainted by time, memories, critical judgement or bad experiences.

As I will detail in the next few chapters, what I have uncovered is not only fascinating, but my first-hand experience, observations, insights and research have also led me to create the framework and founding pillars of WOW, and how we can rediscover this state in adulthood.

There are FIVE reasons why children are masters of WOW:
1. They are natural inhabitants of the present moment
2. They are in an environment of learning, where focus is encouraged and practised daily, and where being creative and making mistakes is expected and encouraged
3. Their natural brainwave state is a state of mindfulness or flow
4. They have an undeveloped sense of self
5. They have a natural sense of awe and wonder about the world

We will look at why children have an unfair advantage over adults when it comes to experiencing WOW; there are internal and external factors which mean that children are both conditioned and exposed to more opportunities for WOW than grown-ups, however we will also consider how we can recreate these conditions in adulthood.

INTERNAL FACTORS

How a child develops; physically, psychologically and emotionally, plays a key role in how easily they experience WOW. During childhood we develop at a faster rate than at any other time in life. At birth, the average baby's brain is about a quarter of the size of the average adult brain. Incredibly, it doubles in size in the first year. It keeps growing to about 80 per cent of adult size by age three and 90 per cent – nearly full grown – by age five.

How a child's brain develops gives them a distinct advantage over adults when it comes to practising mindfulness and finding WOW. Even more interesting is how our brainwaves develop as we grow from children to adults.[1] Children under two years old experience the lowest brainwave levels, **Delta**. These are the brainwaves we access when we are asleep. When we are in this brainwave state, either as a baby, or as a sleeping adult, we are functioning primarily from our subconscious mind.[2] The brain in the Delta state operates at very low frequency and any information from the outside world enters the brain unfiltered without critical thinking, analysis or judgement.[3]

From the age of two years, up until around six years, children function using **Theta** waves. At this age children show very little rational thinking and tend to accept what they are told, and demonstrate almost trance-like behaviour, super-focussed and living in their own world. These are the brainwaves we access when we are in the flow state. When we as adults access these brainwaves, we are our most creative, almost dream-like and totally immersed in what we are doing.[4] In meditation terms, we can access these brainwaves through practising open monitoring, mindfulness meditation.

Children at this age are often absorbed in their 'own little world', which we might use as a negative criticism, but adults might find this immersion somehow aspirational. To take the time to be so engrossed or absorbed in whatever you are doing, that nothing else matters.

What if we could be in our own little world at any given

moment? What would we find? A world filled with awe and wonder, and WOW.

Between the ages of six and eight years, children start to develop their analytical brain and raise their brainwaves to the **Alpha** state. They start to draw their own conclusions and begin to process external stimuli and consider what is happening in their life for themselves. Their imagination is on fire at this stage of their development, that's why children of this age play make-believe and pretend so brilliantly. When we are in Alpha brainwaves as adults, we feel relaxed, happy and focussed. If we practice 'effortless acceptance' meditation, particularly in transcendental meditation, you would likely be in the Alpha state.

After the age of eight, children start operating on higher and higher frequencies switching from low to mid to high **Beta** waves. These are the brainwaves of most adults, most of the time. If you are reading a book on a familiar topic, your brainwaves are in low-range Beta. When you are reading a book studying for an exam, your brainwaves are in mid-range Beta as you are in a state of greater focussed attention.

When using Beta brainwaves, the conscious brain is busy processing, analysing and storing information from the outer world, whilst the emotional or subconscious brain provides us with feelings based on the incoming information.

To access Beta brainwaves during meditation, we would practise a focussed attention technique during which you feel awake, alert and allow thoughts, for example when practising Vipassana meditation.

baby–2 yrs	2–6 yrs	6–12 yrs	12 yrs–adult
Delta	**Theta**	**Alpha**	**Beta–Gamma**
0.1–3 Hz	4–7 Hz	8–15 Hz	16–30 Hz–31–100 Hz
sleep, dreaminess, detached awareness	meditation, flow	relaxation, visualisation	alertness, concentration to peak focus, higher processing

© Lucy Stone

So now we can understand why a child's happiness resides in the here and now, their brainwaves are forcing them to be mindful. They believe every moment is important and deserves to be lived entirely, enthusiastically, fully. There is no nostalgia, remorse, maybe tomorrow or *mañana* attitude.

From teaching mindfulness meditation in person to so many children, I have gained a unique insight into how youngsters access this ancient practice, which so many of us adults struggle to grasp. Although I can teach them specific techniques and give them more of an understanding, children are not taught to be mindful, or to be present in the here and now, they have a natural inclination to want to pay attention to the small things which surround them in that given moment.

The father of modern mindfulness Jon Kabat-Zinn's definition of the practice is 'Focussed attention on the present moment, on purpose, without judgement.'[5] Which could equally have been written to describe what a young child does every day, without even thinking about it.

Very young children have an **undeveloped sense of self**. Ask a young child of around four or five which job they would like to have 'when they are older' you will hear common responses of 'footballer', 'astronaut', 'pop star' or 'inventor'. Very few or any will say management accountant, auditor or lawyer. Primary school children, particularly in the early years before the age of eight or nine will have limitless dreams, uninhibited ambition and a world of possibility. They will have a little or no concept of how difficult it might be to achieve their goals. Childhood dreams are a leveller, they do not yet have the weight or burden of socio or demographic status, they are not pigeonholed to a role or profession and the only version of the self they live by is their own.

They have **no concept of what might be practical or possible for them to achieve**, they have big hopes and dreams and unlimited possibilities. As we grow older, and enter teenage years and certainly early adulthood, we are (sadly) more influenced in our future decisions by the practical realities of where we live, or our background, possibly financial and educational constraints and almost always the opinions of others.

A child's brain is programmed to be mindful; they are natural inhabitants of the present moment which means they find it difficult to focus on more than one thing in any given moment. This leads to another consequence. When they have this super focus on one thing, this thing which is often new and challenging for them, they enter the state of flow, fully absorbed by whatever they are doing in that moment. Linked to this, is the fact that they are unburdened by a sense of self, not looking ahead too far into the future or carrying the weight of the past.

As we will discover in the coming chapters, letting go of our inner critic, our ego, or predetermined sense of self is essential in mindfulness and when accessing the state of flow, both of which are important preconditions for finding WOW.

EXTERNAL FACTORS

Children are in a daily learning environment where focus is encouraged and practised daily. They are fed a diet of just the right amount of age-appropriate content at a time. This gives them time to practise and develop their focussed attention skills and not be too distracted. Although of course this does happen, they are doing their best to stay in control and focussed on the task in hand. They are naturally practising mindfulness, more easily accessing the state of flow and generally finding moments of 'WOW' as they learn and discover.

Furthermore, in this unique environment of daily learning and discovery they are **accustomed and well-practised at making mistakes**. The teacher's red pen, the marks out of ten, the ticks and the scoring are all commonplace, and children understand that this is how they learn. Unlike in adulthood where we maybe have a fear of failing, getting things wrong or being rejected or acting defensively, as children we know this is a daily occurrence.

Another key external influence on why young children are most exposed to WOW opportunities, is that many will **not yet have access to social media**, and perhaps a limited amount of screen time. This helps them to find awe and wonder in simple things.

They have more time for creativity and play, many children's toys such as Lego, jigsaw puzzles and dolls encourage problem solving, creativity and using their imagination. Whereas so much of screen-based entertainment is passive, receiving content and swiping to the next video. Much of a child's play time requires an active involvement.

As children approach the tween and ultimately teenage years, the online world becomes a point of reference. Social media may become more important and along with it, a culture and climate of instant gratification, praise and rewards means that the childhood psyche is altered with peer pressure and judgement. The awareness of the self is born at the same time as the birth of the selfie.

Children find awe and wonder in the smallest of things. After teaching so many children for so many years, I am constantly surprised by what fascinates and inspires children. Sometimes the most seemingly mundane task or activity will become a moment of WOW. Discovering what happens when you scribble black wax crayon over the top of another colour and then scrape it off with a pencil or coin, WOW! Watching a butterfly gently immerge from a chrysalis, WOW! Scoring an incredible goal from the halfway line in a lunchtime game of football, WOW!

When I hear a child's battle cry of 'WOW', I notice the wide eyes, maybe a dropped jaw or perhaps tongue sticking out in deep concentration and engagement with this new experience, and I try and take in some of what they are feeling. These magical moments which so fully absorb and captivate us in childhood but would possibly be overlooked or ignored as adults.

You would think, in a world so full of technology and where everything is available, that modern day children wouldn't be so easily mesmerised by something offline, but if anything, children of the digital age might be more enthralled by these small things because they are a real life, multidimensional experience.

As children grow older, they begin to lose some of the awe and wonder of life. They stop being so interested in wondering about the world, but instead start wondering about themselves and their role in all of this. But the loss of WOW is not just from within, there are certain wow-killers that accelerate the process (more on this later).

THE GOLDEN AGE OF EIGHT

I started this book by explaining that I have taught meditation to over 15,000 children across 60 different schools. These primary school pupils were aged four to eleven, and came from a wide range of demographic and geographic backgrounds. From rural communities to inner cities, children from affluent and privileged families through to young people facing real challenges and from poorer family environments. It is important to note that my observations are true for all children, whoever they are. It is age, not demographic, which affects their ability to be mindful and to experience awe and wonder.

Right in the centre of the primary school age range are those children aged between seven and eight years old. These are what I call the golden years. It is the children in these two school years who without fail, are top of the class in learning the practice of meditation. Of all the children I teach, the most engaging and natural meditators are around age seven or eight. Before this, they are still quite small and can get distracted, after this age they are beginning to be more influenced by peers and finding their place in the pack, with increased self-awareness.

For children around eight, it is less important to analyse what it is happening around them. Instead, they feel and experience the world just as it is, for what it is, seeing the beauty and amazement of the everyday.

An easy conclusion to draw would be that the very youngest, four- to six-year-olds are just getting to grips with the school environment, and the classroom rituals and discipline. Whereas those older children, aged nine to eleven, are becoming more influenced by their peers, and as the eldest children in the school, they are getting ready to 'fly the nest' and move on, and of course we cannot ignore this. But there is something else at play, children aged seven and eight have two additional things going for them, that other children and more importantly adults don't have, which means they can learn meditation easier and are also the WOW-masters.

Firstly, as we have seen their brain development is such that their natural brain waves are aligned with those found when we meditate, so they are already in the right mindset. Secondly, it is well documented in studies of child development that at eight years old, you are said to be your 'true self'. That's to say who you are as an eight-year-old, is the purest version of your personality. These two factors make children of this age the real stars of the show when it comes to learning meditation and are our true inspiration for Find Your WOW.

One summer I was at a music festival, and I observed a little girl of around seven-years-old, head to toe in sparkle with fairy wings, dancing and leaping around, completely lost in the music and the moment, flinging her arms around, jumping and laughing and having so much fun. She skipped over to her tweenage older sister of around 12, who had been looking on and smiling, and asked her to join in, desperately trying to pull her by the arm to dance. The older girl looked around and saw that her little sister was beginning to attract some smiling attention, so refused. The younger sister was truly being her self, without inhibition, full of creativity, absorbed in the flow of the movement. The older sister, although she perhaps wanted to join in, was much more aware of her ego, that inner critic we all hear from time to time; 'what will people think?' 'What if I look silly?'

Before the age of eight, children are happy to immerse themselves in an activity, full of creativity and playfulness, and be purely themselves without even knowing it. After this, so around school year three or four in the British Primary School system; the hands stop going up to ask questions, there is an increase in eye rolling, there is a need to know 'what are we doing next?' There is a looking around the room to gain approval or praise from others and self-awareness, self-doubt, self-consciousness begins to creep in. By the time they hit pre-teen and those golden teenage years, they are being guided and influenced by peers, they are spending more time in the online virtual world and moving from childhood to young adulthood.

Whilst writing this book I was chatting to a friend Niklas over dinner, I asked him if he could remember his eight-year-old self and whether there were many similarities between child Niklas and Niklas now sitting opposite me. Niklas in adulthood, is a senior leader within a global organisation. He looked up from his dinner and smiled, as a memory came to mind. He recounted a time, when he was around eight, growing up in Sweden. He had finished his work in class early and told his teacher, he hoped that he would be allowed outside to play as a reward for being so studious. Instead, his class teacher gave him some extra reading work because he had completed his work so quickly. Eight-year-old Niklas was not happy about this at all. 'How is this fair? I have done exactly as you asked. I have finished my work quicker than anyone else, and now you are giving me more work to do. I refuse!' And with that, Niklas finds a big piece of cardboard as a placard and starts to 'protest' in the classroom, against the injustice of the whole situation. As we laughed at the dinner table, picturing militant little Niklas trying to right the wrongs of his Swedish classroom, I asked him, 'is it true that you were the purest version of yourself in that moment?' 'Absolutely,' came his reply. As a leader now managing teams all over the world, Niklas says his management style comes from two principles: fairness and pragmatism. He detests rules that are in place without any sense and will always try to do the 'right' and fair thing by people.

If only to further illustrate the point, as we left the restaurant late at night, there was a cycle lane adjacent to the pavement. Niklas stepped off the pavement and walked in the cycle lane to take the most direct route 'because it makes no sense to follow the rules at that particular moment as no one is around, due to the late hour'. 'You see,' said Niklas' wife Maya, 'There's eight-year-old Niklas in action again'.

I have since asked this question 'What would eight-year-old you do in this situation?' to a number of friends when they have asked me for advice, and it often throws up an interesting and thought-provoking moment of contemplation. Why not try it for yourself?

What do you think you would have said or done as an eight-year-old if they were sitting next to you right now, what advice would they give you when facing a moment of indecision?

'Show me a seven year old boy, and I will show you a man.'

– Aristotle

In my years of teaching in primary schools, I definitely observed something significant in the children around the age of eight which means they start to lose their awe and wonder, and WOW. As children get older, their appetite grows for 'the next source of entertainment.'

One sunny afternoon I was teaching meditation to a group of ten- and eleven-year-olds. I had taken the session outside as the school had a beautiful woodland area including a pond. It was late spring, and the menagerie of tadpoles we had seen on the previous weeks had grown into substantial sized frogs. The frog chorus was a delight, and I thought their little froggy croaks could become a perfect point of focus for the children. It was a glorious day, and the children were all scattered around the pond on their yoga mats taking in some deep breaths of fresh air and using nature as a soundtrack to their meditation. I was gently guiding them, to 'listen to the frogs' and they were all seemingly in the zone. After a few minutes I noticed one boy was fidgeting and whispering to a friend, so I went over to check he was OK as he was beginning to disturb the class. 'Is everything OK? Can you just take a few moments to enjoy being outside and listening to the frogs?' I said. 'What are we going to do next?' he replied. The sounds of the little croaking frogs just weren't enough for him.

HOW CAN PRACTISING MEDITATION HELP?

We can alter our brainwave state by practising different styles of meditation. Each style has a different effect on the body and mind and can therefore be used for different purposes.

During the day, when we are living and working, we are in the Beta state. This is especially true if we are under pressure or feeling stressed. If your fight or flight response has been triggered, your body produces stress hormones and your brain becomes very focussed on the external environment, expecting to flee from or fight an external threat. When stressed, your brainwaves are in **high-range Beta**. You are too focussed; your mind is too concentrated, and your body is too stimulated to be in any sort of order. These brainwave levels are perfectly normal and necessary when you are facing a life-threatening situation, but can be harmful if prolonged and triggered by everyday situations like a breaking news notification, a stressful email or an approaching deadline.

It would be challenging to experience WOW when we are living in a Beta world. Therefore, we need to find some techniques to alter the brainwaves down to Alpha or Theta. Breathing exercises that stimulate the relaxation response or increase focus can help.

You might practise meditation as a form of 'WOW warm up' to engineer the body and mind into a state where you can cultivate a moment of WOW. By practising mindfulness and meditation, we can increase our empathy, have a slower pace of life, feel a greater connection to others and the natural world, increase focus and attention and lower levels of stress in the body. Therefore, if we adopt a more mindful approach to life, we are more likely to find opportunities for WOW and cultivate WOW-inducing experiences.

When we practise meditation, we often close our eyes, which reduces the information coming into your brain by 80 per cent. By focusing on the breath and shifting our attention inwards, the brainwaves naturally slow down because there will be fewer external stimuli, and you begin to work towards the **Alpha state**. You will analyse less; you will feel relaxed. You will redirect your attention from the external to the internal, each and every time you are distracted. Therefore, techniques like 'counting to ten' and 'taking deep breaths' can calm you down.

The more we focus on ourselves, the more we practise, the brainwaves will slow down even more and eventually enter the **Theta** range. This is when the barriers between the conscious and the subconscious mind are lowered, so you can access and communicate with your subconscious once again. You will be back into the childlike state, aged two to six years old, in your own little world. You are in flow, a world of wonder and WOW.

SUMMARY

In her book The Sense of Wonder, Rachel Carson[6] wrote, 'if children are to keep this inborn sense of wonder alive, they need the companionship of at least one adult who can share it, rediscovering with them the joy, excitement, and mystery of the world we live in.' As adults we can become guardians of children's WOW, and if we choose to experience WOW, we might even become WOW-masters ourselves. Maybe if we start to relive our every day through childlike eyes, we can rekindle some of the benefits moments of WOW can bring.

We have talked a lot about how children are the WOW-masters, and we bow down to their superior talent for finding WOW where others cannot. But our children are growing up in a world filled with distraction, influence and stimulation, and they are in many ways maturing and developing faster than ever before.

The speed of development is so intense from the moment children are born; in a physical sense such as walking and talking, through to learning to read and write through to social skills including relationships, team building and personal confidence. You could say the learning trajectory is almost vertical in childhood, as we grow older it begins to become more of a curve, to the point of flatlining at some time in adulthood. Therefore, introducing new learning experiences in adult life can be an opportunity for WOW. Remembering what we loved to do as children can be a good start, what were our passions and interests? Where did we find joy? Where can we explore challenge and new skills? So many adults have very few, if any, hobbies, those activities aside from work and family which are just for us, where we can be active, creative and playful.

Children can be encouraged and inspired to keep their WOW for as long as possible, parents, carers and teachers are the custodians of children's WOW. We can make time and create environments and spaces for WOW to happen and grow. We can understand that when children and young people are immersed in their learning and creativity, we can keep them protected from the killers of WOW.

By following the WOW framework, you can allow yourself a little patience to pause for a while, to focus without distractions, to be absorbed in the moment, not listen to your ego or inner voice telling you to be somewhere else, doing something else, and just enjoy the awe and wonder once again to find WOW. We can do this with or without a child at our side. Often the simpler the activity, the bigger the WOW. Finding a spider's web covered in dew might trigger more awe and wonder than an elaborate holiday in a tropical location.

What if, for a short while, we let go of that pressure to be THAT person, and found a way to be a more childlike, pure version of ourselves, open to new experiences, or at least experiencing life with new eyes?

'Wonder is the beginning of wisdom.'

– Socrates

Chapter 6.

Introducing the WOW framework

So far, we have examined what children have, which allows them to fully immerse themselves in activities, to enjoy happiness and curiosity in small things and be natural mindfulness gurus. These pillars amount to what I call WOW. Children have WOW, and adults lose it.

It is not our fault that we lose our WOW as we grow older. A combination of factors, including our age, lifestyle, responsibilities and social pressure, our mental and physical health and even where we live in the world can all play a part in determining to what extent and when we lose our WOW.

We have learnt what is at stake when we live in a wow-less world, the effect on our health and well-being, and even the greater consequences on our community and even the planet.

I have identified a framework of how we can rediscover and find our WOW. Not by experiencing the big events in life such as going on an exotic holiday, getting married or having children, but simply by knowing how to maximise the impact of those tiny moments of happiness that occur in our daily lives, if only we stop to notice them. This is what children are masters of, they take the time to stop and notice, to absorb, to be curious, ask questions and learn, to seemingly make time stand still and to say WOW, as often as possible.

What follows is a summary of the WOW framework and an explanation of each of the five pillars. We will then explore each of these in more detail in the following chapters. Helpfully, the WOW journey can be easily remembered by drawing a 'W' shape that you will find below.

Before going any further, it's important to remember that these five pillars are a guide only, and just embracing any one of the pillars will help you towards finding more WOW moments, if you can utilise all five you truly will feel the benefits of a more WOW-full life.

So, without further ado, it's time to Find Your WOW.

The W below is the WOW framework, you can trace the W shape as if it were a path to follow or explore the five pillars individually.

If it helps, picture the W as mountains, high points and summits to reach, with valleys and low points in between. The three high points, peaks or pillars, of WOW go across the top and the two main WOW killers are down in what I call 'the valleys of WOW', which we need to overcome to fully find WOW.

We begin at the top of the first stem of the W, at the first pillar of WOW, NOW. This is the essentiality of stopping to be present in the moment. You cannot experience WOW if you do not stop. This might be stopping in your tracks, a physical halt, or it may instead be a stillness of the mind. You might consider this as mindfulness, but there are a couple more elements required to achieve full mindfulness, which we will explore in the next chapter. But for now, the first essential element of WOW is to stop, and be in the NOW.

If you draw down the first stem of the W you get to the bottom and the first valley of WOW, which is FOCUS. Losing focus, is the first of the two main killers of WOW. As we learnt in an earlier chapter, we are living in a distracted world, and becoming distracted and losing our focus is a huge reason why so many of us have lost the ability to find WOW. We are too busy, distracted or stimulation-blind to notice the WOW beneath our very nose. In a later chapter, we will explore how we can keep our focus and attention easier and for longer, when all around us are losing theirs.

But let's keep on the positive, travel back up the stem of the W to the middle peak and the next pillar of WOW. This is a fundamental aspect of our WOW framework, and one we have mentioned throughout the book so far, FLOW.

Psychologist Mihaly Csikszentmihalyi believes flow unlocks the secret to human happiness and peak performance.[1] It is the mindset cultivated by athletes, performers and many other professionals all over the world. The good news is you don't need to be an athlete to experience flow. It is achieved when there is a natural balance of challenge and skill, and you are pushed to the upper limits of your ability. You may or may not have heard of flow before, but you will have no doubt have experienced it. Some people refer to it as 'being in the zone' where you lose a sense of time and space, you are fully immersed in what you are doing to the point where you think or feel nothing else. There are very strict criteria as to what constitutes you being 'in flow', which we will explore throughout the book.

In the previous chapter we learnt that children are often in the flow state through a combination of their natural brainwaves plus the fact they are constantly developing and learning, they are very often being pushed to their upper limits of ability where their challenge and skill levels are forced, so they learn quickly. Being immersed and absorbed in the moment, to be in the flow state is crucial to finding WOW.

Which leads us down the stem of the W to the second valley and our second main killer of WOW, EGO. Possibly one of the biggest downfalls of being an adult, is the pressure to conform, to be who the world expects you to be. To pretend to be someone you are not. To not be your 'self'. We have already learnt that we are the purest version of our 'self' when we are around eight years old. Before the poison of self-doubt, pressure to conform, feelings of low self-esteem and the self-critic takes hold. One key aspect of finding WOW is to try and quieten this inner voice, the one which says: 'why am I wasting my time doing this? I have seen this all before. I need to get on and do something else'. Or, worst, 'Is that it?'

In this book we will look at ways we can negate our sense of self or ego. To silence the inner critic. When I say ego, I don't mean it in the sense of overinflated personalities or being overly confident. In this definition of ego, I purely and simply mean, our self, who we 'really' are.

Now we draw back up the final stem of the W to the last pillar of the WOW framework, which is to cultivate the conditions for WOW.

Some moments of WOW will be a complete surprise, you might be driving and turn the corner to an unexpected breath-taking view, or if you are travelling by plane suddenly you are above the clouds after taking off from a somewhat grey and drizzly day down on the runway. Or it might be as simple as being captivated in conversation with a friend where you discover something completely new. These experiences might all be completely unplanned, unannounced and to a certain extent they are uncontrolled WOWs.

But once we know where WOWs flourish and bloom and even breed, we can cultivate more of these conditions, so that we can experience more moments of WOW.

As we grow older, our time, our attention, our energy and our resources are spread more thinly. You may have responsibilities; family, friends, jobs and likely, bills to pay. We are working through our days, hour by hour, balancing competing priorities.

What you will learn is that it doesn't take something overly spectacular to be a moment of WOW. Your first challenge is to firstly notice the WOW in the moment, and secondly experience it to its full potential. I aim to help you encounter moments of WOW, whether ones you have cultivated or not, and learn how to make them last as long as possible, to maximise the benefits for your life, health and well-being. You will need to overcome the temptation to become distracted, to keep focussed and fully immerse yourself in the moment, without listening or responding to your inner voice.

The W framework is for guidance, but there will certainly be times when you are feeling overwhelmed, unable to focus, perhaps in moments of grief or deep sadness or don't have the time to dedicate to flow-inducing activities. In this case, you can still try to cultivate conditions for WOW, and then perhaps the rest will follow.

The three peaks to aim for are being in the NOW, being in the state of FLOW and creating the conditions for WOW to bloom. The two WOW killers to be aware of are in the valleys of the W; namely losing FOCUS and listening to your EGO. The five pillars of WOW are not all encompassing, they are not mutually exclusive and can be sought after in their own right.

TO SUMMARISE THE FIVE PILLARS OF WOW:
1. Slow down time, be mindful in the here and **NOW**
2. Increase your **FOCUS** and let go of distractions
3. Access the state of **FLOW**
4. Silence the inner critic, let go of your **EGO**
5. To then ... Find your **WOW**

We will examine one pillar at a time to help you have more moments of WOW and in the process, you might find happiness in the small things, feel better, start to see the world with more awe and wonder and reconnect with who you really are, to help you Find Your WOW which might just save your mind.

© Lucy Stone

You might be thinking; this process is going to take forever. I must stop in the NOW, avoid being distracted and keep my FOCUS, find FLOW, silence my EGO and then and only then, I might just find my WOW. But that's not true, having an awareness of each of the pillars and the process will enable you to engineer more WOW and access those moments more easily. You will start to recognise the opportunity for WOW, even in the mundane and the everyday. And like everything, the more you practise and do this, the easier it will get and the more WOW you will notice.

It becomes a self-serving cycle.

If you happen to experience a moment of WOW naturally, a connection with someone else, a beautiful view for example, you will now know how to amplify and magnify that experience so that you can feel even more of the benefits of awe and wonder and WOW.

By following the framework to Find Your WOW, you will rediscover the awe and wonder of life, just as you did as a child. You might start to see the world differently, which in turn might bring physiological and mental health benefits. You might start to feel more gratitude, empathy, happier and more purposeful. Perhaps you will start to feel more connected to nature and to those people around you, a greater sense of being part of something bigger, whether that is your five-a-side football team, your community or even the planet.

As I am writing this, NASA has just released the photographs from the James Webb telescope which show stars from 13 billion years ago. The images, which show deeper into space than ever before, 'can see backwards in time to just after the Big Bang by looking for galaxies that are so far away that the light has taken many billions of years to get from those galaxies to our telescopes.'[2] When I looked at the photographs and footage, it was a perfect moment of WOW, not just an emotion, but an altered perspective and state of consciousness 'a self-transcendent experience.'[3]

In moments like these, our attention shifts away from ourselves and makes us feel a part of something bigger. Just like mindfulness, and flow, allowing yourself to experience awe and wonder through WOW, which we experience naturally in childhood and can be rediscovered later in life, and with it we can experience some of the physical and mental health benefits WOW can bring. It really can be life changing. But WOW is an approach to life, an attitude, a mindset to be consciously adopted, it rarely just happens.

THE THREE DISTINCT STAGES OF WOW
1. Pre-WOW
This is before a moment of WOW arises.
In this time, you can be:
- Learning and practising the WOW framework
- Working on your mindset for a new WOW order
- Cultivating the conditions for WOW

2. The WOW experience
BANG the WOW is here, it's time to immerse yourself in the moment.

All you can do now is work through the W framework to focus, be mindful, flow and appreciate the WOW, let go of the ego and any distractions and do not, under any circumstances, get out your phone to take a photograph (of course you might!)

3. Post WOW

OK, the moment has gone.

Maybe you've become distracted, you need to go or perhaps the experience has ended.

Now, is the time to try and capture the WOW for future use; to spread the WOW, share the experience with others and save it to the memory bank for a day when you need to live a virtual WOW. This is the moment to take the photo, make a note in the journal or call a friend to tell them all about it.

Take time to reflect, relive, and retell the story of what happened, either in your own mind or with others.

And wait for your next moment of WOW.

'We must remain as close to the flowers, the grass, and the butterflies as the child is who is not yet so much taller than they are.'

– Friedrich Nietzsche

Chapter 7.

NOW

Welcome to the first pillar of WOW, NOW. So, stop right where you are.

Before we go any further, it might be useful to define what I mean by NOW. In order to have a moment of WOW, you need to be 'present'. Or in other words, your mind (as well as your body) needs to be in the 'here and now'.

All too often, when we go about our daily lives, our body is in one place, but our mind is somewhere quite different. It's time to bring them back together. We might be ruminating about the past or worrying about the future, carrying the baggage of memories and times gone by, or mulling over every single scenario of what might happen next, instead of noticing, enjoying and being in the moment we are in.

We are all guilty of this. You can probably remember a time when you were on 'autopilot' whilst doing something; maybe driving a familiar journey, cooking a meal or in a meeting. You somehow completed the task, but have no real recollection of doing so, or any of the details you experienced along the way. Being on autopilot is the antithesis of being in the NOW. If you want to experience WOW, to recapture some of the awe and wonder you have lost along the way of life, you have to be in the here and NOW.

There are two purposes of NOW; firstly, being in the NOW will help you to cultivate more opportunities for WOW, but secondly once a WOW moment comes along, being in the NOW will help you to elongate the experience and make it seemingly last longer, which can benefit your life, health and well-being.

CHILDREN AND ADULTS HAVE A DIFFERENT PACE

I wrote this book whilst teaching mindfulness to children and adults from one day to the next. It became obvious that the rhythm of these two sets of people is very different. Children (although they have times when they run around) are naturally slower paced, they are also living their daily lives on a fixed timetable, both at school and at home and children do not like to be 'rushed'. They like to work at their own pace, exploring, learning and discovering as they go. It is adults who like to, or need to, kill this slow rhythm because we have things to do and places to be.

As we have already learnt, children are in the natural brainwave states of mindfulness and flow, so they find is easier to simply focus on one thing at a time. It is only as we grow older, enter the Beta state and move into the stresses of adulthood that we try and multitask, resulting in our body and mind often being in two places at once.

When children are in the education system, they are in a routine of structured lessons and schedules. During the school day, these timings are set by professionals who understand the capability and capacity of pupils in line with what is appropriate for their age. For example, they will have a 15-minute assembly between 0845 and 0900, followed by English for 40 minutes, followed by music for 40 minutes, followed by a 15-minute break where they will play outside in the playground and have a small snack. They are encouraged to be in the NOW and focus their attention on just one subject and activity at a time, and their brain is set up to be able to do this brilliantly.

As adults we are left to our own devices and set our own pace, rhythm and timetable. We do not have experts guiding us on how many appointments, meetings and activities we should fit in to our day in order to stay productive or healthy. In the name of being efficient, many of us try and cram as much into our diary as possible. Lots of the corporates I was working with described having 'back to backs' (one meeting after another), some even being on their laptop or phone during our mindfulness training, and many not allowing adequate time in their day for eating, moving, 'processing' time between different activities, or importantly – rest.

As we move towards old age, our natural body rhythm and our lifestyle and pace slows down, so we begin to enjoy a slower pace of life once again. As we will discover, in old age our 'happiness' returns to childhood levels and maybe even beyond as we retire and become more elderly. But in middle age, we are at our lowest point on the happiness curve.

As we grow older, as well as becoming happier, we can

have more time to experience things in a more WOW-full way, we are able to stop and look once again, to notice the small details and to be present. This time often coincides with becoming a grandparent, which means we might be lucky enough to have children around us once again, who lead the way and are the WOW-masters.

In this chapter we explore what it means to be in the here and now, how mindfulness can help us, plus many other practical ways to slow down, take a pause and live more mindfully.

Matt Haig's brilliant book How to Stop Time offered one page of simple advice which became a meme and was virally shared.[1]

How to stop time: Kiss

How to travel in time: Read

How to escape time: Music

How to feel time: Write

How to release time: Breathe

The first purpose of NOW is to **slow down** and to be in the moment, which can help you cultivate more opportunities for WOW.

WE NEED TO SLOW DOWN

For many of us, the pace of life is fast and busy, in fact being busy is often proclaimed as a badge of honour. In order to engineer more WOW, the first step might be to try and slow down a little, this gear change and mindset shift might be something you look to adopt in your general life as a rhythm, or you might choose to find those deliberate and intentional moments where you check in and slow down.

HOW DO I SLOW DOWN MY LIFE?

Whether it is healthy eating, exercise or practising meditation, at first it can be hard to install new regimes into your life. People tend to fall into one of two camps. The 'baby steps' camp; introducing little elements of whatever it is you want to change and building up slowly (the couch to 10k mindset). Or conversely, there's the 'all or nothing' camp, where you get rid of all the unhealthy snacks, sign up with a personal trainer and book yourself into a silent meditation retreat to kickstart your new regime.

You might approach Find Your WOW in one of those two ways. Starting gradually, you might want to diarise some 'slow time' each day, or week for moments of WOW. Or you might try to approach your life overall with a whole new way of thinking, a new world, or new WOW order.

BUT REALLY, HOW DO I SLOW DOWN?

Although it is easier said than done to take a slower pace of life, you can simply take more time over everything you do, to allow longer to pause and reflect between activities and to walk, drive or even breathe more slowly.

When we do things slower, we have more time to notice what is happening and process the detail of what is in front of us. We might use more of our senses to hear, smell, feel and even taste what is happening, rather than experience the moment mono-sensorially, with just our eyes. Rather than multi-sensorially using our ears, nose, touch and taste to expand the experience.

We might call this living life more mindfully, but this is separate from having a mindfulness practice.

WHAT IS THE DIFFERENCE BETWEEN LIVING MORE MINDFULLY AND HAVING A FULL MINDFULNESS PRACTICE?

If we live life mindfully, we try and only focus on one thing at a time, to use our senses and notice more details, and fully immerse ourselves in that activity.

Jon Kabat-Zinn gave the following definition of mindfulness as 'Focussed attention on the present moment, on purpose, without judgement.'[2]

If we separate out those four elements:

focussed attention,

present moment,

on purpose,

without judgement.

You can see its link with the WOW framework. The importance of remaining focussed, without distraction. There is an element of intentionality (you are deliberately choosing to do this) and without judgement, would be to negate the sense of self, or inner critic as we have as our pillars.

As we have discovered, children are naturally mindful.

HOW CAN A MINDFULNESS PRACTICE HELP US?

When we adopt a practice of mindfulness, rather than simply living our life mindfully, our brain learns new behaviours in how it responds to different experiences.

WE TALK A LOT ABOUT LIVING IN THE MOMENT. BUT HOW LONG EXACTLY DOES A MOMENT LAST?

I say, a moment lasts as long as it lasts. It is what you make it.

'A moment is eternal.'

– David Hockney

WHAT IS THE SCIENTIFIC DEFINITION OF A 'MOMENT'?

Throughout history, the word moment was used to mean a precise amount of time, which was 90 seconds.

If we consider that a moment lasts as long as a thought, then that would be around 150 milliseconds. For example, it takes a runner roughly that long to process the sound of a starting gun into the conscious action of running. It is believed that our mind's stream of consciousness is composed of individual thoughts flowing in quick succession.

Sometimes we might confuse a moment with a memory, something tangible with a certain time, location and accompanying emotions. Memories are often replayed like movies in the mind, but it will depend on how long your memory lasts, as to the length of the moment.

So, what about the present moment (as opposed to

a memory), how long does that last? The same time as a thought? But in science, the shortest measurable amount of time in physics, is 'Planck time'. Planck time, if we were to put it into numbers equates to **10,000,000,000,000,000, 000,000,000,000,000,000,000,000 Planck times in one single second.**

So as far as physics is concerned, the present moment is pretty short.

If you have ever lived through a scary or dangerous experience, you'll know that the sensation of time can seemingly grind to a halt or move in slow motion. It is not only the negative times, as we will read in the FLOW chapter, when we are experiencing a flow-inducing activity or even just a positive feeling or emotion, time can also seemingly stand still. Do these moments in fact last longer than others, or is it just our perception of them?

But if we just mean the duration of a brief experience, we can at least say how short it can be. In 2014, researchers at MIT showed that the brain can identify images glimpsed for as little as 13 milliseconds.[3]

'The longer you live, the harder it becomes. To grab them. Each little moment as it arrives. To be living in something other than the past or the future. To be actually here.'

– Matt Haig

'Forever is composed of nows. But how do you inhabit the now you are in? How do you stop the ghosts of all the other nows from getting in? How, in short, do you live?'

– Emily Dickinson[4]

What does it truly mean to be in the here and now?
Happiness for me doesn't come from the extravagant, the extreme, the glamourous. It is made up of tiny, precious moments where you are truly present, those moments where there is eye contact, where you feel a sense of connection, where you feel a part of something bigger, where you are grateful, where your senses are stimulated, where you feel love, or loved.

As we get older, we might notice that our perception of time changes. During childhood a summer holiday might feel like it goes on forever, whereas for adults it is over in a flash. Each year I find myself saying 'how can it be Christmas again already?'

In childhood it might have felt that our moments seemed to last longer, and time was perceived differently than in adulthood. For children, most experiences are brand new, and as a result, their brain works overtime to encode as much information as possible into the brain. This creates a form of hyperawareness, where the child is conscious of everything that happens. As we get older and experience more things, our brain starts to create patterns out of all the experiences.

These patterns act like shortcuts and eliminate the necessity to memorise stuff we don't need.

Why does time seem to pass more quickly as we age? One reason is routine. When you're young, you are exposed to more new experiences, which are logged in your memory, leaving you with the perception of lengthened time.

When you do the same thing repeatedly, your brain consolidates the repeated action into one memory, making it seem like time has contracted. That's why you might merge the memory of 261 commutes, where nothing much really happens, into one single memory. But if you go for a long car drive, somewhere you have never been before, then the time will last much longer, and you will have a multitude of memories. If you compare the first kiss you ever had with a kiss in a long lasting or serious relationship, both are kisses, but during your first kiss your brain was hyperaware of every sensation and busily writing it into your memory.

For 'everyday' kisses, your brain uses the mental shortcut and doesn't write it into your memory. Unless you force it to.

Psychologist and time researcher Marc Wittmann[5] says: 'If nothing meaningful has happened, we don't have anything for our brain to record, and time subjectively shrinks.'

You might have experienced this during the pandemic because each day became almost exactly the same, in the same location, with none of the usual entertainments – travel, restaurants, friends and family – that spice up a routine in normal times.

There's not much you can do about the direction in which time moves, but there are ways to slow down the way time feels, so you don't, say, look up in ten months and wonder how your child has gone up two clothes sizes, when you don't remember buying them any new trousers.

15 WAYS TO SLOW DOWN TIME AND BE IN THE NOW
1. **Introduce the slow down.**

Throughout the day, you can weave some 'slow' time where you are in the NOW, these might come from your self-care practices; your shower, eating breakfast, drinking a cup of coffee, exercise, even simple activities like applying makeup or moisturiser. Taking a few extra seconds or minutes over activities and practising some mindful awareness of what you are doing can really make all the difference. Whereas you are normally on 'auto pilot' with little or no connection to what you are doing, now you can begin to feel more present, more aware and using all your senses to be fully in the NOW.

When talking to other people this presents a real opportunity to begin the WOW journey, but this starts with simply being present with whoever you are with. Try and look at them, and most importantly truly listen to what they are saying. This 'active listening' or intentional listening is not the same as just listening, to really take time to hear what the person is saying, to 'hold space' that's to say allow the silences to pepper the conversation so there is room for reflection and respect, without feeling the need to jump in and fill the void. By allowing a mindful conversation to take place, you are respectfully working to a slower pace, and although it might take some practice, if you are used to controlling where conversations go, having a new-found curiosity, and consideration for the other person might lead you to some surprising discoveries.

You can practise this when in conversation with someone. Practise listening to understand, not listening to respond. Finding moments of connection and truly listening to the person you're talking to is a great way to help you slow down and be more present in your life.

2. **De-diarise and be bored. Make breathing room in your day or your week.**

Scheduling in something as simple as a lunchbreak or a few minutes time between appointments. You could even go as far as diarising some time in your week where you can cultivate opportunities for WOW experiences. Simply adding some 'white space' to your diary, can give you some breathing room to help you become more in the NOW.

You might like to start practising some moments of daydreaming or reflection, as little as five to ten minutes of what is called 'mind wandering' (where you allow thoughts to just appear in the mind), stimulates the default mode network in the brain which is the state the brain enters when it is not stimulated.

It's a little like a ctrl-alt-del for the mind and helps gain a sense of perspective on how we are feeling and how we see time.

You might see these moments as 'being bored', but boredom plays a key role in cultivating and creating the right conditions for WOW to be found.

Chris Bailey author of Hyperfocus[6] challenged himself to 'one month of boredom' to rest his brain from overstimulation, he did something extremely bland for an hour every day, from waiting on hold with an airline company to reading terms and conditions. You don't have to go that far, but simple rest and boredom will bring your brain back to that default mode and restore your power to slow down time.

3. **Do something new or challenging.**

This is an obvious one: If routine is a time (and memory) killer, then the best way to change the way you experience time is to break routine. After you've fulfilled your commitments and obligations such as work, family and social life, you can try and make a dent in monotony, by mixing up what and how, where and when you do things.

Psychologist Loren Soeiro[7] says even small changes to your routine can help stretch time. 'There are ways to seek novelty and differentiation, even if they're not expensive or time intensive.' You don't need to go on holiday or go for expensive meals or anything. Just breaking up your workday, going for a walk somewhere new, go out to meet a friend for coffee in the middle of the day. Something that makes it a little fresher.

Other ideas include taking a different route to work, listening to a new album every day, using a lunchbreak to explore a different part of your (or your workplace's) neighbourhood, scheduling novel post-work activities during as many days of the week as you can, learning a new language or instrument, cooking a new meal a few days a week.

David Eagleman, a neuroscientist, says: 'In my mind there is only one way to slow time: seek novelty. The reason this works is because new experiences cause the brain to write down more memory, and then when you read that back out retrospectively, the event seems to have lasted longer.'[8] That's essentially why when you travel somewhere for the first time, it feels so much longer than when you're on your way back. So, to make time last longer, you should push yourself to learn new things as often as possible, or at least trick yourself into thinking something is new, like rearranging your office just to make it feel like a new experience.

4. **Declutter and simplify.**
It is not only important to create space in your diary, but also another simple way to slow down your life is to create space in your home. Fewer things, a more curated wardrobe makes getting dressed faster and easier, so you can start your days with a little less stress and a little more ease. Decluttering rooms, wardrobes and your life mean there is less 'stuff'

around you to demand your attention. Less stuff requires less time, energy and attention to manage it all and having less stuff gives you more time and resources to be in the NOW and find WOW.

Simplifying your life is not just the removal of items, it can be also about getting rid of the non-essential commitments from your to-do list (as we explore in the next point), this can create more time and help you to slow down.

5. **Say 'no' and set boundaries.**

If you can protect your time and are intentional about how you spend it, you will feel like you have more control, and you can perceive time more slowly. Don't say yes to everything and set yourself a boundary of how many commitments you can make each week.

Stress often comes from having too much on your plate, which in turn distorts your perception of time, especially when it comes to work and burnout.[9] But the distortion isn't consistent; stress can make time appear to speed up or slow down, depending on the situation.[10]

6. **Breathe.**

One of the simplest ways to slow down, is by taking some time to sit and notice your breath for five minutes. If five minutes feels too long, try two minutes! When you notice your mind wandering (and it will), return your attention to your breath. Not only are you teaching your brain to be more mindful by returning your focus to your breath again and again, but you are also making an intentional choice to sit and slow down for a few minutes. Which is a great way to practise slowing down in general. This is a form of meditation, but meditation doesn't have to be complicated or intimidating.[11]

One step further, is 'deep breathing' which is another great way to use your breath to slow down. When you find yourself feeling rushed, busy or overwhelmed, try taking three deep breaths, inhaling through your nose and exhaling through your mouth to help release some of the stress and busyness. Try and take this calmer, slower pace with you during the rest of your day.

7. **Be in nature.**
Spending time outside in nature has been shown to have a wide range of physical and mental health benefits.[12] Getting outside can lower your blood pressure, reduce feelings of stress or anxiety, increase creativity and memory, boost immunity and more. But another great benefit of getting outside in nature is the way it helps you slow down and let go of some of the busyness of life. Go for a walk, or even just sit outside for a few minutes.

8. **Move more slowly.**
Intentionally slowing down would seem the most obvious, but perhaps the most difficult way to approach this. By walking a little slower, taking slower and deeper breaths and finding a slower pace to your day, are just some of the ways to weave a slower approach into your life. One of the best

ways I have found is to do this at the very start of the day as this helps keep a slow rhythm throughout the day.

9. **Don't multitask.**

Multitasking is a myth: you're not juggling many tasks at once; you're switching very quickly between tasks. And if you quickly change tasks, you're not really focussing on any of them in a meaningful way,[13] a practice that's bad for your focus and productivity, as well as your understanding of time. We need to stop consciously multitasking. 'This mixes up the energy waves in the brain and creates a sort of tsunami energy effect in the brain, mind and body that will distort our perception of time.'[14] It's no surprise that in a 2015 study, when participants carried out other tasks while watching commercials they felt time was going by more quickly than if they just focussed on the commercials. This is, of course, great for killing time, but detrimental if you're working on slowing your pace.[15]

10. **Enjoy the silence and turn off your phone.**

Technology is a wonderful thing; it makes life easier in so many ways and provides us with many opportunities. But it can also become all-consuming when you're always connected, always reachable, always on, always plugged in. A great way to practise slowing down is by literally unplugging. Turn your phone off for one hour, a whole day, an entire weekend. At the very least, trying silencing some (or all!) of the notifications on your phone so there are fewer dings, beeps and badges vying for your attention. Technology can be a wonderful addition, if we have boundaries to make sure it is adding value to our lives.

Tech can become an unwanted distraction away from the people and activities that matter most, so sometimes simply turning off the literal noise in your life is a great way to slow down and give yourself a breather.[16] Try turning off the TV, music, podcast, radio for a few minutes to give yourself some silence. Take a minute to notice and really pay attention to where you are, what you're doing and what's going on around you.

11. **Use your senses.**

This really works, use your eyes, ears, nose, tastebuds and touch to add a multidimensional element to your life. Keeping an eye out for small changes in your own familiar environment will help break through the routine and bring you moments of WOW.

If you've got plants, keep track of their leaf growth. If you've got pets, teach them new tricks. If you've got children, mark their heights, notice how their face is changing. Note the way the sunlight changes in your living room over the course of the day. These little things make a big difference.

Exercise: The NOW Countdown. One exercise I have developed and used to help children be more present and, in the NOW (something similar is also used in adults' therapy as a grounding technique) is what I call the NOW countdown.

You can hold out your hand in front of you and as you look at your five fingers, then look up and spot five things you can see (starting with something far away, and work closer until 1 is something next to you). Next, you put one finger down and you reach out for four things you can feel or touch. You put another finger down and you listen carefully for three things you can hear, you might want to try and listen for something far away, something closer and something just next to you. You place another finger down and take a deep breath in through your nose and see if you can identify two different smells. And finally, as you put your next finger down, with one finger remaining outstretched, try and identify one thing you can taste. This very simple, multisensory technique is one of the most effective for grounding and being present, and it's beneficial for everyone from children all the way through to adults.

But you don't have to follow this technique completely, simply take some time to savour what you are doing, even if that is as simple as holding your mug of tea. Use your senses to connect to the moment; the smell, the feeling of the warmth, the taste, how it looks, and listen to the sounds around you. And notice if your pace of life feels a little slower.

12. **Practise gratitude.**
Practising gratitude is a great way to slow down and find more enjoyment in life. Not only does it help bring you back to the present moment and shifts your mindset in a

positive direction. The great thing about this practice is it's something you can do anywhere, anytime. Practising gratitude is a great way to slow down and find more enjoyment in life.[17] Not only does it help bring you back to the present moment, but it also shifts your mindset in a positive direction. All you need to do is take a few minutes and think of a few things you're grateful for. Sometimes they are big things, like your health. Sometimes they are small things, like a warm mug of tea.

Shift your mindset towards gratitude to help you slow down and find more moments to appreciate and enjoy in life. Gratitude is a mindset that is often contagious.[18] The more you share what you're grateful for, the more you'll encourage those around you to look for things they're grateful for as well.

13. **Start slow.**

If you can, wake up fifteen minutes earlier, and start the day a little slower. This can have a knock-on effect to the rest of the day, and even if it doesn't, you have just created an extra 15 minutes where you can be intentionally slower. Don't be tempted just to get on with your day in your normal way, use these 15 minutes wisely to connect and welcome the day, maybe using some of the techniques above. Take some deep breaths, have a mindful experience with a cup of coffee or shower, using all your senses. Take a moment to look outside of your door or window and experience some nature (even if it's just looking at the sky), if it's the right time, watch the sun start to rise and remind yourself there's never going to be another day like this one. Perhaps use this time for some quiet time, not feeling the need for extra stimulation from the radio, or music or a podcast. Let your mind gently adjust to this slow simple pace without introducing more 'noise'. Try to let this slow, silent, stillness soak in and absorb just for these first few minutes of your day, try not to even look at your phone (or if you do, don't fall into the trap of falling down an online rabbit hole) until these precious 15 minutes are over.

14. **Make memories last longer.**

Take photos and journal. Consider when and why you take photographs, but also the opposite, when and why you shouldn't. Studies have found that in fact taking a snap of a picturesque view could make our memory of that time worse.[19] Try to build mental images whenever you can, after all, your brain can store up to 2.5 petabytes of data.[20] That's more than 300 years of Netflix, and if you're lucky you'll feel like you enjoyed life for that long. Like journaling, taking photos helps create a narrative record that'll preserve your memories even after your brain expunges them. But don't take too many photos, since studies show that being preoccupied with photo-taking can impair your actual memory of the event you're trying to document, which defeats the purpose.

Your brain might not keep a record of all your repeated memories, but a journal can. If you jot down a few thoughts, feelings and memories per day, you'll preserve those memories before your brain mashes them together and revisiting them later will help you recall time otherwise lost. 'Journaling helps you build up your narrative memory, and your narrative self.'[21] 'It's shown by researchers that when you actualize your memory contents over a certain time span, relatively, time expands.'

15. **Practise Mindfulness.**

In general, being more present makes time slow down, and meditation is a great way to achieve that. Techniques like mindfulness and focussing on breathing help you get 'control' over your perception of time. In addition to expanding your perception of time, meditation can relieve stress and anxiety. You don't need to sit in silence for hours to reap the benefits; there are a number of apps that can assist you in getting started on meditation, even if you can only spare a few minutes per week.[22]

When we live in reaction mode, "time feels like something that is passing us by or we are chasing, a fleeting quality that we are not part of constructing, a cosmic conveyer belt taking us somewhere ahead, forward, toward. Time, when slowed, is spacious. Time when contracted or ignored is not, and we become 'pressed for time'."[23]

MINDFULNESS HAS A MULTITUDE OF BENEFITS BUT WHEN WE ARE CONSIDERING 'NOW', THESE ARE:

- A mindfulness practice will help you to keep your focus and attention for longer
- Feel gratitude more deeply and greater connection to others and the world around you (e.g. the natural world)
- Help you to regulate a slow rhythm (you will be less inclined to rush)
- Put the brakes on your natural flight and flight response which is stimulated when we are in a stressful situation, mindfulness helps you to feel physiologically calmer (e.g. lower heart rate, blood pressure and stress and anxiety levels)
- Helps you to think more clearly with clarity and gain a sense of perspective (we are less inclined to multitasking)
- Through neuroplasticity, mindfulness can change neural pathways and alter our behaviour and reactions. (So, once we have found our new, slower more WOW-aware life, it will mean this will become our default action, so we are less inclined to go back to rushing, busyness without noticing the details of the world around us.)

'To talk about memories is to live them a little.'

– Matt Haig

My meditation teacher once said: 'Meditation is not about having a particular experience, it is about noticing what the experience is.'

By using some of the 15 ways to be in the NOW not only will you be priming yourself ready for WOW experiences, which are all around us, but also when you realise you are in a moment of WOW you can use some of the techniques to make the experience last a little longer, which can benefit your life, health and well-being.

'It is not the skills we actually have that determine how we feel but the ones we think we have.'

– Mihaly Csikszentmihalyi, Flow

Chapter 8.

FLOW

As you move through the WOW framework you are beginning to see that each of the pillars offers opportunities for WOW moments to be cultivated proactively, but also how WOW experiences can be extended and deepened.

After years of research, alongside my classroom observations, I have learnt that the state of flow is very important when it comes to finding WOW. In previous chapters I started to explore flow, which experts say is the optimum mindset for happiness and peak performance.

We have learnt that from two to six years, the brainwaves of children are naturally in this state (Theta), which means they are living their everyday life in flow, enabling them to easily be able to immerse themselves in whatever they are doing, without distraction.

BUT WHAT IS FLOW?

Just think for a moment, when was the last time you felt so focussed and immersed in something you were doing, that you lost all sense of time? Maybe you were spending the morning working in your garden, and before you knew it you had weeded through lunch, it's 3 pm and you wondered why you were suddenly hungry. Perhaps you were out walking in the countryside and realised you hadn't really thought about anything for a while, just simply – walked, for hours. Or what if you were playing your favourite sport and you were so absorbed in the game, time felt like it had stood still. In these moments, you were likely in a state of flow which has some similarity to mindfulness.

WHERE CAN I FIND FLOW?

There are set, prescribed conditions for when flow technically arises, which I will explain. A flow-inducing experience doesn't have to be an activity where you are particularly, well, active. People find flow, and along with it find creativity and problem-solving solutions, in all sorts of situations. From brainstorming ideas in a creative meeting, cooking a meal, playing sports, working through a complicated spreadsheet... and there have been so many of life's problems solved in showers.

How many times have you been ruminating on a situation, idea or complex problem, you go for a walk and bang the solution or idea comes to you? Similarly, many people have their best ideas when they are driving or commuting to work. Often when we take ourselves away from the situation (in this case maybe sitting at your desk and staring at a computer screen), we are refreshed and more open to a new way of thinking and viewing the world, which can be incredibly creative and helpful.

THE LINK BETWEEN FLOW AND WOW

FLOW, like NOW, has two main purposes in the WOW framework.

Firstly, by taking part in flow-inducing activities and allowing yourself to enter the flow state you will find you are likely to have more moments of WOW because you are fully focussed, immersed and absorbed, plus, you will be pushing yourself to the outer limits of your ability.

Secondly, by accessing the flow state regularly, you will be able to drop into flow, or 'the zone' more easily, and thus enjoy a greater immersion when you are faced with a WOW experience. Research tells us that the more we access the state of flow, the more easily we will be able to access it. The practice of accessing flow is a self-fulfilling cycle. Much like WOW.

WHAT IS HAPPENING TO ME WHEN I AM IN FLOW?

Neuroscientists have discovered that when we are completely immersed in flow, hormones are released, creating Theta brainwaves, which are conducive to the flow state. The neocortex in your brain ramps up dramatically, increasing the speed at which you learn, and the prefrontal cortex temporarily shuts down (the part of the brain responsible for what are called 'executive functions' such as planning, decision making, short-term memory and expression of our personality).

This is why when we are in this state, we seemingly lose a sense of ourselves and a sense of time. These are the neurobiological conditions which make creativity and peak performance readily available to all of us, children and adults alike.

In this chapter we will discover; what are the conditions for flow, the benefits of accessing the flow state for our health, well-being, personal, creative and professional life, why FLOW is in the WOW framework and explore some techniques for how you can easily access this state in your everyday life.

THE CONDITIONS FOR FLOW

The conditions for flow were set out by the Father of Flow, psychologist, Mihaly Csikszentmihalyi[1] (Pronounced: Me High Cheeks Send Me High) who describes those moments where you feel 'in the zone' or completely absorbed in a challenging but doable task, when your skill level and the challenge in hand is matched.

'The best moments in our lives are not the passive, receptive, relaxing times… The best moments usually occur if a person's body or mind is stretched to its limits in a voluntary effort to accomplish something difficult and worthwhile.'

– Csikszentmihalyi

He concluded that the flow state experience was comprised of eight key dimensions:

1. You have clarity of your goals, there is immediate feedback;
2. There is a transformation of time (speeding up/slowing down);

3. You are completing the activity with effortlessness and ease;
4. There is a balance between challenge and skills;
5. There is a feeling of control over the task;
6. You have complete concentration;
7. Your actions and awareness are merged, you lose 'self-conscious rumination'
8. The experience is intrinsically rewarding;

This is the strict criteria for accessing FLOW, but the last three points are particularly relevant when looking for WOW:

1. You have complete concentration on the task (You keep your focus, you are in the NOW)
2. Actions and awareness are merged, losing self-conscious rumination (A lack of EGO)
3. The experience is intrinsically rewarding (WOW moments are reward in themselves)

THE REWARD IS THE EXPERIENCE

When we take part in an activity or experience something which is a reward in itself, we do it purely for internal gratification, without any need for external praise, this is called an **autotelic experience**. We will learn more about this later in the chapter.

Mihaly Csikszentmihalyi[2] was a keen mountain climber, and often spoke about finding flow as he climbed, but also described a certain amount of disappointment when he reached the summit, as the experience was over. In our

WOW framework, we aim for an engaged absorption in what we are experiencing, when finding your moments of WOW try not to seek out any reward, gratification, or praise, but just enjoy the awe and wonder of the experience itself.

IT DOESN'T HAVE TO BE PHYSICALLY CHALLENGING

It is important to note that you do not have to be partaking in a particularly extreme challenging or difficult activity to access flow, what is important is that you are controlling your focus to absorb yourself in the moment.

Can you find flow by just looking at a view? You might have recalled previous moments or experiences where you have said 'WOW', but it was when say, you turned a corner and you were faced with an incredibly beautiful vista, and you might be wondering; 'How on earth do I access the flow state when looking at rolling hills or a lake?'

Here's how. Imagine a situation where you have said 'WOW', the view has taken you by surprise and you are enthralled by its awe and wonder. The challenge here is to 1) not drive on, 2) remain focussed on looking and be present in the moment, 3) notice all the details of what you are looking at, 4) use all your senses to bring that experience to life; the smells, the sounds, the textures and even the tastes. In fact, you are using the view as inspiration for a mindfulness practice.

Mindfulness is a useful skill to learn when it comes to flow. When you practise mindfulness, you access the brainwaves of the flow state, so it is in itself a flow-inducing activity.

Furthermore, when you adopt a mindfulness practice, it helps retrain the neural pathways in the brain, through neuroplasticity, that enable you to access flow more easily in other areas of your life such as when playing sports, at work or even in your relationships with other people.

If you stand and look at the view, you may have the feeling or sense that you are a part of something bigger. As we have learnt in previous chapters, this is a key element in the science of awe and wonder, as well as flow. People often describe feeling to be in a state of flow when they are at a music concert or performance, when they are part of a crowd with incredible stimulation and multisensory elements to the experience.

You don't have to be skiing down a mountain at 30 km per hour to experience flow, you can simply be on the mountainside looking at the view.

THE NECESSITY OF THE PERMISSIVE MINDSET FOR FLOW
As I touched upon here, on the journey to finding your WOW, there are going to be choices and decisions to make. If we take the example of driving along a road, you turn a corner and stumble across an incredible rolling vista or view (perhaps you can picture one now). If you consider that as a busy adult with 'lots of things to do' and 'places to be' and your opinion is 'one view looks much like the other, we have seen mountains before' – several things might happen at this point.

At one extreme, the result is that you will not notice the view at all. Or perhaps you take a fleeting glance at the view, you say 'WOW' to yourself, a feeling of awe and wonder washes over you and lasts for a few seconds, until you turn the next corner, and the view is gone.

Possibly, as soon as you say "WOW" you realise this is an opportunity for something greater and longer-lasting. You look for a safe place to stop the car, you park and get out to take in the view for a few minutes more. You make a commitment to experiencing the WOW for as long as possible. You pause, and try to be in the moment, you focus on the view, taking in as many details as you possibly can, using all your senses to build the picture. You breathe in the fresh air, you have a sense of connection to nature and something bigger, you don't feel the pressure to be rushed and you absorb the moment for as long as you possibly can. Then, you might take a photograph on your phone to help relive the memory later, or even share the WOW with others by sending them the picture message. As we will learn later, WOWs can be experienced virtually not just in real life, but I always say that your personal WOW moment comes first, to experience it in real life before it becomes a virtual commodity.

Ethan Hawke in his wonderful TED talk, 'give yourself permission to be creative' talks about having a permissive mindset.[3] This goes for all the pillars of the WOW framework; NOW, FLOW and cultivating the conditions for WOW. As adults we have many competing diversions for our time, energy and resources, it takes a whole world of effort, commitment and permission to grant yourself the time for WOW.

HOW DO WE ACCESS THE FLOW STATE?

It might be an easy way out to say: 'you will know it when you feel it' and the likelihood is of course we might just feel it when it just happens, we might know how to get into the zone, this optimal state of mind where we feel and perform our best, but essentially you are looking for opportunities which are ripe for Mihaly Csikszentmihalyi's eight conditions for flow to flourish.

When teaching mindfulness to children and young people, I explain about the benefits of accessing the state of flow for exams, sport and other areas of their life. I have developed an acronym to help them access flow more easily, which I will share with you now.

Focus your breathing and your attention in the moment

Let go of inhibitions, distractions and let your imagination run wild

Observe your surroundings to flow more easily

Work out (move) and wind down.

These four different ways to access the flow state and to develop your own flow strategy start with mindful and focussed breathing. I recommend the box breath technique which is to breathe in for a count of four, to hold the breath for a count of four, exhale for a count of four and hold the breath again for a count of four.

As you are exhaling the breath, try and let go of any tension or persistent thoughts, and begin to just let your imagination become free, allow creativity to begin. If you find mindful breathing a little tough, get yourself outside and start to focus on the natural world around you, perhaps the clouds in the sky, the leaves on the trees or listening to the sounds of birds singing.

You can use any or all these techniques as a little flow warm-up before starting out with your fully chosen flow activity, it might help the transition from your every day, alert and distracted mind to become a little more focussed, a little sooner.

HOW TO KILL YOUR FLOW
As we will learn in the coming chapters there are two main killers of WOW which also kill our flow. The first is lack of focus. You can't experience flow if distractions disrupt the experience. The second way to slide out of flow is when your inner critic comes out to play, or your perception of the challenges and skills in front of you are out of balance. So don't try and experience something too difficult, or too easy.[4]

Focus is more than just completing one task at a time, not being distracted is one thing, but the quality or depth of your focus is another. Sophie Leroy in 'Why is it so hard to do my work?'[5] describes an effect she called 'The attention residue' which is when you switch from Task A to Task B your attention doesn't immediately follow – a 'residue' of your attention remains stuck thinking about the original task.

THE LINK BETWEEN FLOW AND EGO

I mentioned the 'L' part of my acronym above, is Letting go of inhibitions, this will be explored a little more in our EGO chapter next. When you are in a state of flow, your inner critic is silenced, you are in harmony with yourself, you use all your senses to lose and immerse yourself in your experience. You somehow feel and see nothing and everything all at the same time.

Mihaly Csikszentmihalyi found that some of our happiest moments are when we access a state of flow. When we lose ourselves for a while, lose all track of time, are fully immersed and absorbed, nothing else seems to exist or matter. You are not thinking about any end result or praise you might receive; you are just enjoying the experience. You may even have feelings of being a child once again, without a care in the world. You feel carefree, your mind is uncluttered and, dare I say it, you are happy. Children are lucky in that they can access this state easily, freely and regularly, they lose themselves in whatever they are doing, and this goes hand in hand with the ability and appreciation of being in the present moment, the gateway to mindfulness.

HOW LONG CAN YOU REMAIN IN THE FLOW STATE?

Research shows that to access that ultimate peak performance state of flow we need to remain focussed for around 90 minutes, beyond that we need to take a break. It takes around 15 minutes to get into our flow state and we peak at 45 minutes. If anyone distracts us or interrupts us, we reset the clock. So, you can see how living in a distracted world can kill flow and thus kill our WOW.

HOW HAS FLOW BEEN USED IN THE PAST?

Throughout history the very best 'genius minds'; inventors, scientists, authors and musicians have accessed flow as an essential part of their work for creative inspiration and innovative thinking.

When we access the flow state, we are leveraging from the Alpha (mindfulness state) and Theta brainwaves (the natural brainwave state of two to six-year-old children). The benefits of accessing these 'magic' brain states were found by scientists and inventors, long before MRI and CT scans could measure them scientifically.

In the 19th century, one of history's most prolific inventors, Thomas Edison, was able to intentionally access the flow state to leverage his creativity and innovation. Edison invented the incandescent light bulb and motion picture camera as well as making huge improvements to the telegraph and telephone and he once said, 'My so-called inventions already existed in the environment, I've created nothing. Nobody does.'

Other inventors had already made huge roads into the development of the light bulb. But Thomas Edison's gift, was not so much inventing but perfecting. Edison did not look for problems in need of solutions; he looked for solutions in need of modification.

Edison was a master of surfing between the Alpha and Theta states and had a technique for accessing the flow state for creativity, without moving very far at all.

Edison would sit in his armchair in front of the fireplace. Once comfortable, he would cradle ball bearings in both hands with brass plates on the floor below. Then he would start to drift off to sleep. When he loosened his grip on the bearings, they would fall and strike the plate, which jolted him awake. He would then reset and repeat the process.

As his brain made new connections, Edison avoided falling asleep. In that state he chewed over ideas while semi-alert. With this practice, Edison 'rode' the slowing brainwaves into Alpha and Theta states which as we know are associated with creativity and higher learning. Edison's strategy for problem solving relied on relaxation rather than stress.

Researchers studying sleep suggest that Edison might have been on to something. One study[6] reports that we have a brief period of creativity and insight in the semi-lucid state that occurs just as we begin to drift into sleep, a sleep phase called N1, or nonrapid-eye-movement sleep stage one. The findings imply that if we can harness that liminal haze between sleep and wakefulness – known as a hypnagogic state – we might recall our bright ideas more easily.

In the hypnagogic state we have already dropped beneath our Beta (everyday alertness or adulthood) brainwaves, and are free-falling fast through Alpha, these are the mindfulness brainwaves where we begin to feel present and relaxed. When we are in this sleepy trance-like state, we are moving from Alpha to Theta (the brainwaves of flow) where our creativity, imagination and inspiration lies.

However, we are riding what I term the 'sleep train' at this point. If we fall beneath Theta, we are into Delta state and we will be fully asleep.

Other examples of genius whilst in the flow state include Surrealist painter Salvador Dalí who used a variation of Edison's method: he held a key over a metal plate as he went to sleep, which clanged to wake him as he dropped it, supposedly inspiring his artistic imagery.

Albert Einstein went on daily walks to find his flow, while inventor and physician, Nikola Tesla insisted on squeezing his toes 100 times a day, which he said, 'stimulated his brain cells' and enabled him to access flow.

All these inventions, discoveries and creative sparks would have without doubt been moments of WOW for these geniuses as they experienced them. Flow enables us to experience WOW, but also helps us to become more focussed, absorbed and a part of WOW moments which arise.

CAN ANYONE ACCESS FLOW?

You might think the flow state is for the geniuses, the elite, the musicians and the athletes, but this is not true. We all have the same basic tools, we have the same brain, and the flow state brings out the best in all of us. But if we are all wired in this way, do we just wait for it to happen, or can we turn it on? And can we forget how to get into it?

Diane Allen,[7] a professional violinist and TED speaker talks about **finding a flow strategy** and she encourages you to

ask yourself these questions:

1) Where are you mostly when you experience flow?
2) What are you doing there?
3) Why are you doing it? What is your purpose?
4) And how can you reframe or repurpose this for other areas of your life?

THE FLOW CYCLE

For decades it was thought that 'being in the zone' or accessing the 'flow state' was an on and off switch. You were either in flow or out of it.

In his book The Rise of Superman, Steven Kotler[8] developed what he called the 'flow cycle' which is the journey we all travel through in our pursuit of flow. He says because humans do not understand how this cycle works, we are unable to access flow fully and properly and therefore not truly able to reap its awards and benefits.

To summarise Kotler's theory, the four parts to the cycle are struggle, release, flow and recovery. The first stage of the flow cycle is struggle, which seems like it would be the antithesis of flow. This is when you are working hard, training, researching, preparing or purely and simply finding the chi or motivation to even attempt your flow-inducing activity. This might be when you must make that decision to get out of your warm and cosy bed on a wet winter's morning to go for a run, or to set aside some time and open the laptop and start to write that book. In this stage you are overloading the brain with information, and many people will fall at this first hurdle.

The second stage is release, or relaxation. This is when you take your mind off the problem by perhaps going for a walk, having a snack or taking a break. It is essential to rest the brain at this point. So many people fall at this hurdle, by either not taking a break and burning out or undertaking some activity (such as watching TV or going on social media) which does not relax the brain, and distracts us so we do not return to the original activity.

It is only during stage three of the cycle, which we recognise as the true flow experience, where the magic happens, everything suddenly feels effortless, you are performing, and in flow. It feels almost like an out of body experience and time just passes. As we have learnt in earlier chapters, you cannot stay in the flow state forever. Some researchers think that it is a maximum of 90 minutes before the peak benefits of flow begin to dwindle, but many argue it is much less than this.

Then we move to the fourth and final stage of the cycle, consolidation. Here there is a downside. As you come down from the high of the feel-good chemicals released during flow, you will go on a down which might lead to self-sabotage or some other reaction to try and regain the flow state. Some people might see this stage as a sign of failure or allow the stress to block the learnings and memory of the flow experience. But after a rest it is completely possible to restart and repeat the cycle once again.

BENEFITS OF FINDING FLOW

Research has primarily focussed on the experience of flow within structured leisure activities such as sports, education and creative arts.[9] When we consider its place within the Find Your WOW framework, it is important to recognise the role it plays within many other aspects of life including a route to well-being.

Experiencing flow is an important predictor of emotional well-being.[10] It plays a huge role in subjective well-being[11] and in the relationship between well-being and healthy aging.[12]

15 WAYS TO FIND YOUR FLOW

We can experience flow in almost any activity where the eight conditions for accessing the flow state can be found. Most importantly where there are clearly defined goals and a balance between your perceived level of challenge and ability.

1. Competitive activities. Whether that's playing in a team sport or an individual activity such as playing computer games, any situation where there is an element of competition is a perfect hunting ground to find flow. People report experiencing being in the zone or accessing the flow state within sporting activities more commonly than in many other contexts.[13]

2. Flow at work. We have all had those days where your workday drags and you 'clock watch' every single hour ticking by. But perhaps you have experienced the opposite, where you have been so absorbed or challenged by a task that time just flies by. It may seem unlikely, but the workplace is not too dissimilar to playing sports or video games. At work we have targets, deadlines and goals, immediate feedback and the skills required to complete a task.

Researchers have found that accessing the flow state has many benefits within a workplace setting,[14] for example it encourages productivity, creativity and cultivates innovative thinking.[15]

One way you might be able to find flow at work is to try taking on a challenge you haven't attempted before or ask your employer to trust you with an important task – by taking a calculated risk where you know your skills are suited to the task you can push your limits and achieve flow.

McKinsey Quarterly: '… Most report that they are in the zone at work less than 10% of the time. (But) if employees… are five times more productive in flow than they are on average, consider what even a modest 20-percentage-point increase in flow time would yield in the overall workplace productivity – it would almost double.'[16]

3. Creative pursuits. Whether it is playing a musical instrument, sketching or painting, modelling with clay, dancing, or writing in a journal. Creative pursuits are a great place to find flow. What's more, when we find flow in a creative activity, we might find inspiration for other areas of our life, for example problem solving on a personal dilemma or help with clarity on decision making.

Music, whether that is listening to or playing, is often a place where we can experience that sense of complete absorption.[17] If we think about a musical performance, the orchestra knows exactly what they are doing in the moment, they seem to flow together, the players are completely absorbed in the music with their intense concentration allowing them to enter a state of flow.

Taking a break from the mundane to engage in creative activities you find enjoyable can boost self-esteem, increase motivation[18] and enhance well-being.[19] So why not reacquaint yourself with the joys of downtime, pick up a musical instrument, learn to knit, take up photography or try your hand at painting or writing? Kotler suggested that creativity can trigger flow and in turn, flow increases creativity in a positive feedback loop.

And don't necessarily think of creative pursuits in purely the creative arts. Think of how you can bring an element of creativity to your cooking, baking, gardening or even DIY around the house. Remember that finding flow is about stretching your abilities, using your imagination, problem solving, taking risks, failing and learning, growing in confidence and believing in yourself. Not listening to your inner critic, not being distracted and remember that you are doing this just for you, for no other praise or feedback or verification.

4. Flow in technology. [My teenage son will be delighted that I have included this suggestion.]

For many of us, technology can be used, or support us to experience the flow state. Researchers[20] found the emergence of flow during gaming was in part due to the balance between the ability of the player and the difficulty of the game, concentration, direct feedback, clear goals and control over the activity. Furthermore, game designers Jenova Chen and Nicholas Clark developed a simulation game called 'Flow'[21] based on Csikszentmihalyi's flow theory, wherein the game automatically adjusted its difficulty and reactions based on the actions and skills of the player. Through this personalised challenge-skills balance, less skilled players reported an increase in control and felt more immersed in the game and more able to achieve flow.

Some studies have shown that flow is experienced frequently while performing a variety of technology-based tasks ranging from word processing, programming, visual design, animation, photo editing and online searches.[22]

Watching television or films might be relaxing, but it is not considered that we access the state of flow in these circumstances as we are a passive observer, not actively taking part.

I want to make one note that while technology (whether that is gaming, social media or other apps) can be flow-inducing (with all its benefits), can very quickly become a source of addiction, which is for the user to be mindful of. Unlike any of the other suggestions I have listed here, technological outlets have been specifically designed by the best psychologists and developers with the sole purpose of keeping you engaged, absorbed and stimulated. But you probably knew that already.

5. Learn something new or within an education setting. Csikszentmihalyi suggests the end of formal education should be the start of a different kind of education that is motivated intrinsically.[23] Finding interests or areas of study to immerse yourself in in adulthood can help not only with self-development and self-improvement but also finding flow.

In recent times, (especially during the pandemic) e-learning has become increasingly popular with online courses and workshops popping up on every subject imaginable. Learning something new is a perfect flow-inducing environment, with a clear set of goals to achieve, which you work through at your own pace within your skill level. The amount of effort, motivation and focus we put into our learning will determine if and how deeply we access flow.

So why not think of something you have always wanted to learn; a new language, a skill or craft or perhaps a class you can enrol in at your local college or university. Finding new opportunities to challenge yourself is a great way to access the flow state, and with apps and the online world full of learning resources, you might only be one click away from finding flow.

6. Autotelic activities. This perhaps is one of the most important ways to find flow, and I would also suggest for finding WOW. In case this is a new word for you, autotelic activities are those we do for their own sake, where simply to experience the activity is the goal itself.

The word combines two Greek words 'auto' meaning self, and 'telos' meaning goal. Our old friend Mihaly Csikszentmihalyi in his own words said: 'An autotelic experience is very different from the feelings we typically have in life. So much of what we do, is because we have to do it, or because we expect some future benefit from it.' A side effect of an autotelic experience is we can focus on the process, the moment, the journey – instead of the destination. It's harder to find the curiosity and focus in the here and now if your attention is pointed towards a later external reward.

Activities are never fully autotelic or exotelic, but often a merger of the two. For example, if you love your job and would do it even if you were not paid, in reality you still need to make a living out of it. Vincent van Gogh, when embarking on his artist career, did not sell a single piece of his work for almost a decade. He didn't even begin painting until he was 27 years old, but he never gave up. He was on a path of curiosity, discovery and learning new techniques.

Finally, the day came when he had sold a painting, his brother Theo contacted Vincent to give him the great news. Vincent, however, was a little non plussed and is rumoured to have said: 'You know there are fireflies in Brazil that are so luminous that in the evening ladies stick them into their hair with pins. It's very fine, fame, but see, it is to the artist what the hairpin is to those insects.' For Vincent the act of painting was reward in itself, an autotelic experience, and for this reason the commercial reward was not important.

In the summer of 2022, after the pandemic lockdowns and restrictions, I went to a concert of one of my favourite artists; the Tallest Man on Earth. He was overcome with emotion to be performing in front of a crowd again as he said when he performs music is when he feels most alive. He described that during the pandemic he was living on a farm in Sweden and how, to get his 'performance fix' he had been playing and singing to his horses and other animals. Truly autotelic.

Our hobbies and interests might be examples of autotelic activities; we all have something we are intrinsically motivated to do regardless of external rewards. Creating 'Art' for the sake of it, reading a book, restoring antiques, plane and train spotting (I am a big fan of Francis Bourgeois – look him up on YouTube if you haven't seen him), dancing in the kitchen, bird watching are all examples of autotelic activities, where you might just Find Your WOW.

'You need not see what someone is doing to know if it is his vocation. You only have to watch his eyes; a cook mixing a sauce, a surgeon making a primary incision, a clerk completing a bill of lading, wear the same rapt expression, forgetting themselves in a function.'

– WH Auden

'A little kid's life bursts with autotelic experiences. Children careen from one flow moment to another, animated by a sense of joy, equipped with a mindset of possibility... They use their brains and their bodies to probe and draw feedback from the environment in an endless pursuit of mastery. Then – at some point in their lives – they don't. What happens?'[24]

7. Activities which focus on your body. When you feel a connection between your body and mind, you are more likely to access the flow state. We have mentioned that playing sports often induces flow, as well as other movement such as walking or dancing.

But one group of activities deserve a special mention, those which involve mindful movement such as giving a massage, practising yoga, martial arts or activities such as Tai Chi. The latter is often referred to as 'meditation in motion' and is known to enhance overall connection, well-being and encourage a relaxed state.[25] Through physical action and the achievement of a meditative state our concentration is focussed, and our mind becomes clearer.

Activities such as these help to ground you in the moment and teach you to control external distractions, so that you become more aware of sensations within your body. These activities are ideal for people who prefer low impact exercise.

8. Activities which focus your mind. Csikszentmihalyi suggested the normal state of the mind is chaos and whilst it is relatively easy to concentrate when our attention is structured by some external stimuli, when left to our own devices the mind reverts to a disordered state.

We will learn that the two main killers of FLOW and WOW are distraction (loss of FOCUS) and our inner critic (EGO). Therefore, activities that help maintain our focus and attention can be flow-inducing; examples might be playing chess or card games, mindfulness and other meditation techniques. The brain's natural tendency is to ruminate and focus on the negative, so we can try to use the power of the mind to regain control and steer our thoughts in a positive direction.

To practise mindfulness and other styles of meditation is a great way to access the flow state as well as improve our focus and attention, increase our creativity, and it helps to calm and relax the body and mind.

Taking time to rest and deeply relax is an incredibly worthwhile activity and one where you can access the flow state in a non-physically active way. If it's good enough for Edison and Einstein it's good enough for us; being relaxed or even on the verge of sleep is a perfect hunting ground for the flow state and all that follows. Whether that is through mindfulness, rest or other techniques, when we are relaxed, we are more likely to find flow. One simple breathwork exercise to remember is to double the length of your exhale to your inhale. For example, if I breathe in for a count of four, I can breathe out to a count of eight. This simple process stimulates something called the relaxation response within the brain which helps rebalance the body and mind into a more relaxed state.

9. Mind wandering. Although many of the examples so far of where you might be able to find flow have involved being proactive and some form of physical activity, this one requires you to seemingly do absolutely nothing.

Whenever I travel by public transport, especially the train, I love to just look out of the window. One of my favourite pastimes when I am on holiday is to sit on a café terrace with a cappuccino and watch the world go by. I am not really thinking about anything, I am just allowing my mind to wander. Sometimes I am daydreaming, but I am letting my thoughts flow.

Whenever I do this, I have the sense that I am so 'lost in thought' that time seems to alter. Daydreaming can be a place to find flow, and there are similarities between the two practices, but they are not quite the same. In both flow and daydreaming you might experience the feelings of being completely involved, focussed and concentrated and unaware of the passage of time as well as feeling like you have somehow been transported outside of everyday routines. However, the conditions of flow around achieving or creating something which pushes us to our outer limits of ability is perhaps not so similar. Daydreaming may help us with that creative block or problem we want to solve, and it might also serve the purpose to improve our mood or help us to relax.

The autotelic enjoyment of thinking, rather than there being any reward that would be gained by it, is just a wonderful thing. If, however, I am sitting in an exam room, trying to remember the facts and figures from my revision, these couple of hours thinking time would be very different experiences. Being bored isn't so bad after all.

As a child, I grew up in the screen-free Somerset countryside with only what I could find as my entertainment. My days were filled with imagination and games, fresh air and nature. I can't really remember being bored. And if I was, this was not thought to be a bad thing.

Being bored is good for us, in an 'always on', overstimulated and distracted world, it gives our brain time to rest, reset and relax. It can help us to alleviate stress, become more creative and use our imagination to think in different ways. Boredom or apathy can play a part in the journey for flow.

Which leads us to our final point on mind wandering. When we allow our mind to wander without purpose or agenda, we might find that we are leveraging memories which can assist in flow state achievement, particularly if it involves recalling the fulfilment of a goal and the positive emotions that accompanied it. By reliving previous successes, we can assess our skills in relation to the difficulty of a task and set appropriate goals which meet the challenge-skill balance required to achieve a flow state.

10. Communication with others. Communication, whether it is talking in conversation or writing, is another way of encouraging flow. Being inspired, learning from others or improving our understanding of past experiences are all opportunities to flow. This is when 'active listening' or mindful conversations come into play. To allow the conversation to flow and resist the temptation to blurt out whatever has come to mind, trying to connect with our conversation partner, when it would be rude to interrupt.

Communications don't have to be spoken of course. You might find yourself in a state of flow when crafting a written letter or email, or perhaps even in text or message conversation on your phone.

11. Join a crowd. The flow state is more than just an individual phenomenon. Research has shown that there is potential for group flow to enhance a team's effectiveness, productivity, performance and capabilities.[26] 'There can be no genuine creativity without failure, which means in turn there can be no group flow without the risk of failure.'[27]

Moreover, it has also been shown that you can experience flow when simply in a crowd, for example at a music concert, a protest march or sporting event. The qualities of intense concentration, clear group goals, communication, familiarity and equal participation (equal skill levels within the group) can magnify flow within a crowd, team or group. (More on this later.)

12. Pushing yourself out of your comfort zone and taking risks. Consider trying an activity or experience which has some perceived physical, mental, social or emotional risk for you. If you push yourself out of your comfort zone (but not so much that your challenge-skills balance is upset) it will help you focus and achieve flow. Routine may be the cornerstone of productivity, but it is not the cornerstone of flow.[28]

Immerse yourself in new experiences and environments – unpredictable situations make us pay more attention to what is happening in the moment. Why not try playing a new sport or joining a different social group?

Take part in activities that have high consequences for you personally – whether they are emotional, intellectual or social risks, try pushing yourself to achieve things you never thought possible. Too intimidated to speak up in that meeting? Clear your throat and go for it. Never enjoyed running? Sign up for that couch to 10k.

13. Setting goals. These don't have to be big or life-changing targets, but you might find flow by setting yourself simple goals such as learning one new recipe each week to add to your repertoire. You might consider, 'What do I want to achieve this day, this week, this month, this year?' You could write these down in a diary or journal and what is important is that you do not look for external validation, instead rely on your own internal validation, the goals you have set and achieved are enough to legitimise your success.

14. Being in nature. It is when I am in nature that I can find flow most readily. Walking in the countryside, on a beach or in the mountains and using all my senses to absorb a multidimensional picture of my surroundings. Being in nature forces me to look closely at what is changing around me, if I have walked in this place before, what is different. The changing seasons are a constant reminder of the ebb and flow of life, which fills me with a childlike awe and wonder. I am curious to learn about what I am seeing, hearing and experiencing. What is the wildflower? Why is that cloud formation that way? Which bird's song sounds like that? How old is that tree likely to be? What was this field used for in years gone by? Is it really true that this beach was once the seabed, how many millions of years ago?

I have two types of 'Flow walk' to share with you. Firstly, the 'new walk', this is a fairly easy way to find flow as I am absorbed by new, challenging and different surroundings.

However, the second 'Flow walk' might sound strange, as it is the 'same walk' in the same place that I do almost every day. Just at the bottom of my road is a beautiful cemetery where many of my local dog-walking and history-loving community like to visit. Not only are there some fascinating gravestones steeped in history and stories of the past, but there are woodland sections, open fields and little pathways to explore. Without a word of a lie, I walk this walk at least once each day with my cocker spaniel, Barney. It's one of his favourite places in the world. Because this place is so familiar to me, I do not need to think about where I am going or where I am walking, I can simply immerse myself in the experience and my natural surroundings.

How is this possible? Because I am WOW-ready, I am open to it, I am hungry for it. I walk pretty slowly; I am in the NOW. Whatever has happened that day I try to leave it at the cemetery gate and take some time away from everything. I occasionally listen to music, but more often I listen to the natural sounds around me, my phone is in my pocket, no distractions or notifications, I am looking around. I am looking up at the sky, I am looking at the trees, I am reading the names on the headstones, I am watching out for wildlife, the birds and my particular favourite, the Jay.

I am connecting and engaging with Barney my dog. I notice if anything has changed with the seasons, or if anything new has appeared since the last time I was there. I don't always take the same route around the paths, but I know how all the paths are linked so I don't need to worry about getting lost, I am able to flow. I use all my senses; listen, smell, touch, feel, look around me. If my inner critic says I should go somewhere new or get home to start work or make that call while I am walking, I silence it by giving myself permission to have those 30 minutes just for me, and every single day without fail I will have at least one moment of WOW. I feel relaxed, in awe of nature and reconnected with the rest of the world. These little walks each day have kept me sane, and I have started to see the world differently. By finding WOW on my doorstep, I have a greater appreciation of the beauty in the simple things in life, I find joy in the mundane. I have a greater connection to the planet, my community, a slower pace of life. I am happy and I am healthier.

Whether I go there at sunrise, lunchtime or sunset, I treat the walk as a completely unique adventure. I force myself to see what has changed from the last time I was there, the beauty in what is around me, to almost feel like I am becoming a part of the place. Some of my most creative ideas, problem-solving thoughts and inspirations have been experienced here. I think there might be something special also about walking amongst the graves of for example, a little slave girl who was transported on a ship to Bath, just up the path from Queen Victoria's chief physician who is a stone's throw from the three immaculate rows of 30 identical white headstones of soldiers who died in the First World War aged between 18 and 45.

**Death, like flow, is a leveller,
it comes to us all.**

One Norwegian entrepreneur, coach and creator of 'Slow Business' Torill Wilhelmsen uses walking as a form of meditation.[29] Torill specifically encourages people to walk the same walk regularly which forces a practice of looking at what is new, and I completely subscribe to this thinking. A fellow Bath author, Garry Pratt in his book The Creativity Factor[30] uncovers how spending time outdoors can fully harness your creative potential.

One of my favourite composers, Ludovico Einaudi took the same approach with Seven Days Walking[31], a series of seven albums released over the course of seven months illustrate his same walk, seven different times. Einaudi describes his walks in the Alps, which 'always follow more or less the same trail.' He revealed that during the heavy snow, where he could not see so clearly, his 'thoughts roamed free inside the storm, where all shapes, stripped bare by the cold, lost their contours and colours,' allowing him to construct the 'musical labyrinth' present on the records. The composer also took a series of Polaroid pictures, inspiring him to write seven volumes of music, each portraying a different aspect of his journey.

'In the mountains of Switzerland, I had time to focus. In one sense I had a clear direction, but I was searching for a direction too. Your mind starts to wander. Where is the final point? It became a kind of meditation. My thinking was completely free.' He was inspired, by the tight, repetitive structure of the mountain tour he'd created: the walk became a journey of the mind. 'Some people prefer to change location all the time,' he says. 'But even as a child, I did the same walk to school, with little differences, and I enjoyed the repetition. Within the familiarity you notice the changes; the weather, the light, the people.'

Einaudi in one interview encouraged people to walk without headphones, and to focus on the moment; using all senses to absorb, engage and interact with everything around you and to have a perfect moment to think creatively when you are walking.

15. Spend time with children. After all, they are the experts.

MAKE TIME FOR FLOW

One technique which has been used for finding time in the day for flow and to maximise your time in the flow state, is the Pomodoro technique. While this doesn't work for everyone, if ever you find temptation in procrastination, you might find it a useful way to achieve focus in short bursts.

The premise of this technique is simple: set a timer – usually for 25 minutes – and focus solely on your task intensely during that time. When the timer is up you should have a five-minute break before you set another timer. While some may find that this technique obstructs the flow state through interruption, for others it helps gain focus and loosen up.[32] Other hacks for finding flow include finishing writing mid-sentence, Ernest Hemingway loved to stop when he was on a roll and suggested to always stop when you are going good and when you know what will happen next. If you do that every day, you will never be stuck. Don't think about it or worry about it until you start to write the next day.

PARTING WORDS

Flow is a state of complete absorption which, according to Mihaly Csikszentmihalyi, produces the highest level of human happiness. It comes about when you are doing something which is difficult enough to require all your concentration and effort and skill, but not so hard that it defeats you. Because that activity takes everything you have got, you have no time to think about all of life's worries and the thousands of thoughts which enter your head each day. You are simply thinking about this one thing. You are your best, most authentic self. In flow, a person is 'completely involved in an activity for its own sake. The ego falls away. Time flies. Every action, movement, and thought follows inevitably from the previous one. However, wherever and whenever you find flow, your whole being is involved.'

GO WITH THE FLOW

In an over-diarised, overstimulated, distracted world, I probably could have written a book entirely on flow and the wonders and benefits of being in that state. I could argue that as grown-ups we have lost our ability to flow, and to a certain extent we have. But of course, I have given you some techniques and hacks to find this crucial part of our WOW framework.

But as a parting remark, I have something I would like to share with you. If I think back to the 15,000 children who are my original inspiration for this book, one of their attitudes to life when they are given the freedom to do so, is spontaneity.

When my son was younger, if I asked him a question, he would often reply, 'Why not?'

Meaning, 'Yes, unless there is a reason we shouldn't?'

Me: 'Shall we go to the park Fred?'

'Why not?'

Me: 'Do you fancy trying mushrooms for dinner?'

'Why not?' (He still doesn't like mushrooms ten years later, and won't even really try them now.)

These two simple words 'Why not?' became a little

catchphrase for him, and a little mantra that I began to try and adopt for myself whenever I could. Saying 'Why not?' when the inclination might be to think of all the reasons why I shouldn't do something became quite liberating.

Taking this to the extreme, journalist and author Danny Wallace wrote the book Yes Man[33] in which he said 'Yes' to every question, offer and invitation for a year. 'Probably some of the best things that have ever happened to you in life, happened because you said yes to something. Otherwise, things just sort of stay the same. But the happiest people are the ones who understand that good things occur when one allows them to.'

There is beauty in allowing things to flow, to be spontaneous, to see what might happen if you don't do anything at all. To say yes, whenever you can and your boundaries allow, and by not being in control of every micro moment of your life, or maybe even the lives of those around you. By allowing life to flow just a little more for many of us is a mindset shift, which might encourage opportunities to flow and Find Your WOW.

Throughout history and in philosophy, people have written about the necessity of giving up control. Carl Jung for example said, 'One must be able to let things happen'.

In the Taoist philosophy which emphasises living in harmony with the Tao; (generally defined as the source of everything and the ultimate principle underlying reality), there is a concept called **Wu wei** (in Chinese: 無為). This has been described as the art of 'not doing' which is definitely not the same as 'doing nothing'. 'If we have to translate it, wu-wei is probably best rendered as something like "effortless action" or spontaneous action.'[34]

So maybe one of the best ways you can Find Your WOW is to allow life to flow just a little more. We might not be able to control everything that happens to us, but we can control how we respond and react.

'You cannot control the behaviour of others, but you can always choose how you respond to it.'

– Roy T Bennett

'You may not control all the events that happen to you, but you can decide not to be reduced by them.'

– Maya Angelou

'You have power over your mind - not outside events. Realise this, and you will find strength.'

– Marcus Aurelius

'Life is a series of natural and spontaneous changes. Don't resist them; that only creates sorrow. Let reality be reality. Let things flow naturally forward in whatever way they like.'

– Lao Tzu

'See the world through the eyes of your inner child. The eyes that sparkle in awe and amazement as they see love, magic and mystery in the most ordinary things.'

– Henna Sohail

Chapter 9.

Cultivating the conditions for WOW

Let us now explore how we can cultivate the conditions for WOW. Even if you apply all the other pillars, of being present and mindful in the NOW, being truly FOCUSsed on what you are doing, finding the state of FLOW and negating your EGO, what if you still don't truly find a moment of WOW?

I think it is important to remember that even if you are working through all the other pillars, these are beneficial practices to bring to your life for your health, happiness and well-being. What we are really looking for, and the premise for this book, is this additional awe-inspiring element, that openness to learning and discovery, the willingness to be surprised and enthralled to be WOWed.

This chapter is about laying the ground for the seeds of WOW to grow and bloom. By cultivating the right conditions, we can maximise our chances of finding WOW. We will explore the overarching themes for opportunities to find WOW, and in a later chapter, Good WOW hunting we will examine some specific examples of potential WOW-inducing experiences you might like to consider.

There are ten overarching themes on how you might Find Your WOW:

1. LEARNING AND DISCOVERY

When we are at school, one of our main jobs is to be taught, and to learn. After we leave school, the opportunities for learning are not so structured and often come from ad hoc and self-induced learning.

Children are in a daily environment set up for the very purpose of learning, whereas in adulthood it will very much depend on our chosen path, and our own individual mindset which will determine how many opportunities to learn we will encounter each day. Aside from the physiological and psychological growing we might have from childhood into old age. As adults we continue to be problem solving, adapting and sensemaking which requires an incredible amount of energy and brain power.

By the time we are five years old, 85 per cent of our brain is developed.[1] Recent research has found that children and adults exhibit differences in a brain messenger known as GABA, which stabilises newly learned material 'making learning more efficient in children than adults.'[2]

The early years are the most active period for establishing new neural pathways in the brain, but we continue to form new connections into adulthood. We can even intentionally alter these through neuroplasticity.

As adults, we often face situations where we are forced

to change, and for many these periods of transition and transformation don't come naturally. The Kübler-Ross change curve[3] provides an overview of the state of mind adults go through and is a powerful model used to understand the stages of personal transition.

After an initial phase of denial, a period of frustration and depression sets in as we are filled with doubt about how to adapt and find a way forward. With time, a phase of acceptance emerges, which starts with experimenting and generating new ideas and options. A problem-solving stage follows, where we start to let go, accept change and learn to work with the new situation. Finally, changes are integrated and embraced, and the individual begins to apply learnings and rebuild their way forward as a renewed person, even seeing benefits coming through with the changes.

As children we are primed for learning and discovering WOW experiences, as adults we may have fewer opportunities for learning, however we can put ourselves in the best position, the right places, with the people, for WOW to happen. We will explore more of these specific ideas and examples later in the book.

2. EXPERIMENTING AND FAILING

The pressure to be perfect, right and not fail is huge in adulthood, which might mean that we rarely experiment, or try new ways of doing things. The fear and cost of failure means that we might take the safest option, whereas a more experimental approach could result in innovation or a more creative solution.

Thinking of ways you can experiment without fear of failure, might mean you experience more moments of WOW. The brilliant Elizabeth Day's podcast How to Fail[4] is full of inspiring stories and interviews of people who talk about how their 'failures' have shaped and affected their lives.

'Most of the old moles I know wish they'd listened less to fear and more to their dreams.'

– Charlie Mackesy, The Boy, the Mole, the Fox and the Horse

'Fail Fast, Learn Fast, Improve Fast' coined by the Spotify Engineers, might be wise words to live by, so go on, experiment, try, fail, what is the worst that can happen?

3. CREATIVITY
As adults we often develop the fear of the blank page when it comes to creative pursuits.

Whether it is writing, sketching or dancing, we are frozen in fear to even begin.

To be the first on the dance floor, to add the first brushstroke to the canvas or type the first words of the sentence. Children rarely experience this barrier, for they are keen to get started and often show unbounded creativity. We need to examine and try and eliminate this fear when it comes to finding our WOW.

The autotelic nature of flow and WOW is important to keep in mind, this means that the activity you are doing is a reward in itself, without looking for perfection, feedback, praise, critique or reward.

Creative pursuits are brilliant opportunities for WOW; even (especially) if you do not consider yourself to be particularly artistic, musically gifted or creatively minded, there are ways that we can use these activities to be mindful, access the flow state and find WOW.

When we access the flow state, if we can keep focussed, negate our ego, inner critic and sense of self, we might find that we are in a moment of WOW. This is particularly the case when we are on the edge of our 'Flow corridor' when we are really pushing ourselves to the limits of **what we perceive we can do**. This is when you are most likely to experience WOW and feel that moment of wonder.

Whether it's dancing in the kitchen to a song that you love or seeing a watercolour you are painting come to life on a blank canvas, maybe you're learning an instrument and eventually manage to play a bar of music after you've been practising for hours, or you hold up a sweater you've be knitting row-by-row for months, and it's finally ready to be worn by someone you love. All these moments of WOW are there for the taking, we just need to make time.

If you can engineer any opportunities to be unapologetically creative, get out the paints and canvases, learn a new craft, buy a block of modelling clay and start to mould, and see what happens.

4. PLAY

In a similar vein to creativity, children love and are experts at playing. Whether it's a physical game like 'tag' in the school playground at breaktime or creating an imaginary world under a blanket den in the living room or role-playing characters in a make-believe story. There is no limitation to their imagination and ability to play.

Ask a group of adults to do any of those playful activities, and you will get some confused and fearful looks. Play drops from our radar in late childhood, often never to return. And with it some incredible moments for WOW.

Let your inner child be free, try not to let your inner critic extinguish your playful spark and allow your imagination to run wild. Any opportunities to be playful whether in sporting pursuits or creating fun and playfulness in your everyday life may well present surprising and WOW-inducing times.

5. USING OUR SENSES

When we are running on autopilot, we often do not allow our senses to be heightened and to see life through a technicoloured lens. Cultivating conditions where you can use all your senses to add colour, and flavour and texture to experiences, can also cultivate the breeding ground for WOW.

When Marcel Proust[5] eats the madeleine dipped in lime blossom tea it triggers a process of bringing a memory to life. The 'madeleine moment' or Proust effect is 'the ability of a memory to be invoked involuntarily when it had been previously blocked.' The act of dipping the madeleine took

Proust back to his childhood, to a happy memory, magnified through the taste of the simple madeleine and the lime blossom tea. When this moment occurred, Proust would have likely been stopped in his tracks, (NOW), completely focussed and immersed in the experience (FLOW), using all of his senses, would have said 'WOW' or 'Wouah' in French. This story serves as a reminder how smells, tastes, sounds, images, even textures can bring up moments of WOW from our childhood, so we can relive them as adults.

You may also find that blocking out one or more of your senses, heightens the others, for example having a feeling of weightlessness when floating in a saltwater tank, and I explain more in my 'Good WOW hunting' chapter about when I visited a restaurant where you sit in complete darkness for your meal.

Thinking about how you can cultivate moments where you can feel a sense of the sound, taste, sights, touch and smell around you, might also bring about a moment of WOW. Food for me, is a huge area of WOW, the perfect combination of a feast for the tastebuds, nose and the eyes. More than that, I am often in complete awe and wonder of the talents of the chef to be able to create something so magnificent. If ever you watch cookery or food programmes on television (Stanley Tucci's series on Italian food is one of my favourites) upon tasting the culinary delights, WOW is often one of the most common responses.

In the contemporary science of consciousness, sensory qualities that accompany an experience including those referring to food, are called 'Qualia'. The term refers to the sensory experience: the redness of red, the fragrance of a rose, the coolness of water are all examples of qualia. How qualia arises from the activities in the brain is one of the great unsolved mysteries of neuroscience. What gives us pleasure is a mystery of science, and life in general. By releasing our own burden of 'self', enables us to open an infinite world of sensory experiences and pleasures and WOW.

6. OUT OF YOUR COMFORT ZONE

In the FLOW chapter we learnt there is a set point in any activity where your challenge and skill level are balanced, and you can access the flow state. Scientists and researchers believe that to really experience optimal flow (and I believe to cultivate the conditions for WOW), you need to be pushed out of balance, and have a challenge which is just slightly out of your ability range. This is an area of growth, sense of achievement and very often, WOW. Thinking of opportunities where you can push yourself out of your comfort zone, may mean you can cultivate conditions for WOW experiences. This doesn't have to mean big and life-changing moments, for example attempting a half marathon when you are only ready for a 10k, but what about saying 'yes' to an opportunity deep down you think you can do, if only your inner critic wouldn't be so vocal and plant seeds of doubt in your mind.

You can probably think of an example right now. My advice? Try it and see if you can find a moment of WOW right there, what is the worst that can happen? Why not get together a group to attempt it, to give yourself courage and create some strong bonds.

7. SOMETHING NEW

As children, we have new experiences each day; learning new things, going to new places, finding new ways to look at the world. Cultivating conditions for WOW is often about trying to recreate this feeling of newness, just as we did as children. Looking for new experiences, is often the easiest ways to engineer moments of WOW. This might be as simple as going to a new restaurant or different supermarket or visiting a friend who has moved to a new town or trying a new sport or activity, rather than a new and exotic holiday destination. But any new experience, taken with the WOW mindset can be rewarding.

'I've never had a coconut chilli Martini before,' I tell him. 'That's the thing with getting older. You run out of new things to try.' 'Oh, I don't know,' he says, still the optimist. 'I have lived beside one ocean or another most of my life and I have yet to see the same wave twice. It's the mana,[6] you see. It's everywhere. It's never still. It keeps the world new. The whole planet is a coconut chilli Martini.'

– Matt Haig[7]

Have an awareness of how doing something new makes you feel. Try to reframe nerves as excitement, but try to experience the new, with a childlike awe and wonder, with curiosity and it might open a whole new world.

8. NEW WAY OF DOING SOMETHING OLD

It is not possible to do new things all the time. Look at what you do regularly, in your everyday life, and think of new ways to do the things you do every day or week, as this is also a fertile ground for moments of WOW.

We know that it is all too easy to be on 'autopilot' with familiarity. An advantage of having an experience we have had many times before is we will be doing it with a certain amount of ease, which will enable us to access the state of flow more readily. A lot of our life is made up of repeat actions, often mundane tasks and familiar ground, so if you can find your WOW here, then you're on to a winner.

This might be as simple as shaking up your routine, maybe changing the time of the day or even time of the year you experience things will bring new experiences and help you to see things differently. If you are an after-work jogger, maybe switch it to a sunrise experience, or maybe go for a swim rather than a jog instead. If you always visit Aunty Flo in Durham at Easter, maybe see the city in a different season and go in October for a change. Finding a new route to work or to visit friends, to look around more and use your senses, to use a new recipe for the staple meal you cook each week, to rearrange the furniture so you have a different view from your favourite armchair, to speak to neighbours you would normally ignore, to mix your seeds or bulbs in a bag and plant them randomly so when they appear in spring, there is an element of surprise. The list is endless, and we explore more ideas in Good WOW hunting.

Throughout his life, Albert Einstein would retain the intuition and the awe of a child. He never lost his sense of wonder at the magic of nature's phenomena – magnetic fields, gravity and so much more. He retained the ability to hold two thoughts in his mind simultaneously, to be puzzled when they conflicted, and to marvel when he could smell an underlying unity. 'People like you and me never grow old,' he wrote to a friend later in life. 'We never cease to stand like curious children before the great mystery into which we were born.'[8]

9. MAKING TIME

As adults, we often plan and diarise our schedules, with little or no room for spontaneous experiences and last-minute events to appear. Leaving white space and clear time in the diary is a start and to not fear the chance to be bored or uninspired. It also gives you the opportunity to say yes when you are invited to something unplanned. You might find that freeing up time is one of the greatest gifts you can give yourself, time for creativity, learning, spontaneity, exploration, discovery and without question, moments of WOW.

Slowing down time is important. When we rush, we are not in control, and we fail to be in the moment. Make time for your own small rituals which allow you to slow down and be in the moment. For me, it is as simple as making a cup of tea. To enjoy all the steps, to be present and take what I call a mini break for the mind, every time I put the kettle on.

10. CONNECTEDNESS

Look for experiences where you can feel connected or part of something bigger, to have a sense of community, to be close to other people and the planet. 'Social connectedness' is a state of feeling close or 'connected' to other people. This includes feeling cared for by others, and caring about others, as well as a feeling of belonging to a group or a community.[9] Surround yourself with good friends, invest in friendship and being part of society, give back to your community, build trust and give each other courage and emotional safety, share moments of WOW with friends. Happiness and purpose are only possible as a connection with others.

In cultivating the conditions for WOW, you are not only shifting your mindset but also perhaps your routine and some of the basic cornerstones of our life. You do not necessarily need to do all these things, but just beginning to add a few of these conditions might give some moments of WOW to bloom and materialise.

Remember there's no guarantee for WOW. You could think that you have set the ideal setting/circumstance for engineering a WOW and then, nothing. And this will happen. It might be for a whole world of reasons, but what is important is to continue to practise, and chances are the WOW will arrive when you least expect it, like so many things.

The more you practise, and have your eyes open for

a WOW experience, the more you will have them. It's like anything, say you are thinking about buying a VW Beetle, the chances are you will suddenly see so many more VW Beetles on the road. Or if you are thinking of going to Paris on a mini break, you will suddenly be inundated with Paris-related imagery or information. Social media and internet search history algorithms aside, what you are seeing as 'signs' is in fact your conscious awareness being heightened, the anterior insular cortex part of your brain acting as a gate for conscious awareness.[10] So, in much the same way, the more you are open to WOWs, the more you will see.

And more than that, when following the 'W' WOW framework, of being more mindful, trying to keep focussed, allowing the flow state, letting go of your ego and inner critic, this will become a thought pattern of behaviour. And through an incredible process called neuroplasticity your brain is literally rewiring itself to be able to spot and notice WOWs. Your brain is having a WOW 2.0 update, right in front of (or rather, behind) your eyes.

'Everything distracted me, but most of all myself.'

– Patti Smith

Chapter 10.

The killers of WOW: FOCUS

As we have already learnt, we are living in a distracted world, and more to the point, we are living in a distracting world. We are surrounded by temptation, notifications and stimulations which are bidding for our focus and attention every waking minute. Everything is available at any time.

From the moment you wake up, every single second of your waking day your eyes will give the brain the equivalent of 10 Mbits (binary digits) of data. We have an orchestra of soundwaves taken in through our ears and we are thought to have around 6,000 thoughts per day.[1]

Many people I spoke with when I was researching for this book, described that their focus had been particularly affected during the COVID-19 pandemic; piles of half read books, working from home meant 'procrastination cleaning' and multitasking rather than finishing tasks, many said their attention had become foggy and it was miserable.

When we consider FOCUS within the WOW framework, I have identified the absence of focus as one of the two main killers of WOW. When we are faced with a WOW-inducing experience, a lot of the effort and challenge comes from trying to stay present in the moment, to try and access the state of flow to become fully immersed within the experience, and to stop any external or internal distractions.

WHAT DO I MEAN BY EXTERNAL AND INTERNAL DISTRACTIONS?

If we start with the **external**; these are all the outside competing factors for your focus and attention, some of which you can control and some of which you cannot. These might be anything from; the people you spend your time with, through to the notification settings on your phone, to the level of volume on your car radio. Anything at all which is external to your body and mind.

By limiting the number of distractions around you, or perhaps more importantly, understanding the level of distraction which works for you, and setting your own boundaries is important. As I mentioned there will always be distractions which arise that we cannot control, but so many of them are completely under our domain. In just a moment, I will talk about how we can deal with distractions and thoughts that are seemingly out of control, as there are ways in which we can eliminate or certainly dial down the impact of these too.

Internal distractions are the ones going on inside your body and mind. Most likely these will be your thoughts, emotions and sensations. As we will learn in the next chapter, this links to our second main killer of WOW, EGO.

Ego is so important as a WOW-killer it needs its own

chapter, as you will read more later in the book. Incredibly, up to 95 per cent of our thoughts are repeat thoughts, which means we have had that thought before, and even more astonishing is that more than 70 per cent of our thoughts are believed to be negative.

Other internal distractions might include the pace at which you live your life, for example if you always feel like you need to rush because your diary is full, and finally your mindset of permission.

You can limit and deal with distractions as and when they arise, which is my main learning from my mindfulness practice over the past 20 years.

'One of the biggest freedoms you have in life is how you react to things.'

– **Charlie Mackesy**

However well we set ourselves up to remain focussed, whether that is on a task at work, or to attempt ten minutes of uninterrupted mindfulness meditation, or simply focus on a WOW-inducing view, we are human beings and prone to distraction, thoughts and self-talk. What makes us different is how we respond to those distractions.

I AM GOING TO BUST A FEW MYTHS NOW AROUND MINDFULNESS

As humans we cannot, ever, empty our mind completely. We are continuously exposed to distractions, thoughts, feelings and emotions.

So here are three simple truths I would like to set out before we go any further.

1. It is impossible to empty your mind and remain focussed at all times
2. Having an awareness of when a thought has distracted your attention is key
3. How you respond and deal with the thought and loss of focus is the differentiator

You can learn to overcome the WOW killer of lack of FOCUS through simple exercises, and crucially through practising. There are a few **standout techniques** that have served me well in my own practice, and in my teaching of children and adults over the past six years.

The first is the simple mindfulness technique of **labelling**. Whether you are sitting down for a meditation, working at your computer screen, or faced with a WOW experience, you want to keep your focus for as long as possible and not let a lack of focus kill the moment.

Whenever you notice that your mind has wandered, and you want to keep your focus on what is in front of you, you can say, 'I have noticed that thought, that thought is [insert label], I let go of that thought.' The mere act of observing the thought and releasing it without engaging and getting into conversation with it, is not only liberating, but it will also keep your focus on the moment for longer.

There are other techniques for improving focus and eliminating distractions, but for me this simple mindfulness labelling technique is the very best, and what's great is that anyone can use it from four to 104 years old.

Your focus resides in the brain, fuelled by glucose, it's sometimes easy to forget that the brain is an organ that needs energy, support and care to perform at its best. You cannot just decide to have undivided attention, you need to practise having an awareness of when you are distracted and learn to observe rather than react.

Dr Amishi Jha's book Peak Mind: Find your Focus, Own your attention[2] prescribes exercises to strengthen attention. One of her techniques involves sitting upright, closing your eyes and focussing on where your breathing feels most prominent, usually in the chest or diaphragm. Direct your focus here like a beam of light and notice when thoughts or sensations pull it away. It might be a memory bubbling up, a reminder that you need to reply to a text or an itch. So long as you notice when the **'flashlight'** moves, then moving it back. That's it.

I have two more techniques that I have used in my mindfulness teaching to help with focus. The first is the **'body scan'** where you lie down, or sit, and use your focus to move through the body, from your toes to the crown of the head, you are encouraged to notice what physical sensations are there. Whenever the mind wanders, return it to the area of the body where the attention was before the mind wandered.

And finally, as mentioned earlier in the book, the **box breath technique** where you breathe in for a count of four, hold your breath for a count of four, breathe out for a count of four and hold your breath for a count of four and repeat as many times as you feel you need.

Developing a mindfulness practice not only gives you practical ways to focus your mind when you are distracted, but also improves your overall focus and attention through neuroplasticity, which reprogrammes the neural pathways and connections in the brain. Mindfulness training helps us direct attention to where we want to focus instead of leaving our brain to control us.

THE IMPACT OF STRESS ON YOUR FOCUS

The WHO reports that stress is the epidemic of the 21st century and it is also one of the biggest killers of FOCUS. When we are stressed, we are more easily distracted and we might have feelings of brain fog, irritability and overwhelm.[3] Amishi Jha states that when we are stressed, our body and mind is on high alert, and in the fight or flight state. We often start overthinking, ruminating and catastrophising. Sometimes we get stuck in 'loops of doom' or imagined scenarios, and this impacts our 'working memory' (the amount of information which can be held in our mind at any one time). This is why we feel brain fog when we are stressed. She further highlights it is easy to become controlled by our thoughts: 'Wherever it is that attention goes, the rest of the brain follows. It means that where you pay attention, makes up the moments of your life, it makes up your life's experience.' There is a condition called 'Easily distracted anxiety' and the symptoms include:

- You have difficulty concentrating and your mind constantly drifts from what you were focussing on
- You have more difficultly forming thoughts and staying on track than normal
- Your thinking feels muddled and impaired
- You feel as if your short-term memory is not as good as it normally is

The more we know about the brain, the clearer it is that **stress** is the **enemy of concentration**[4] so finding time to do the things which alleviate stress; get enough sleep, eat well, relax, can help and with luck, the focus will follow.

What is happening in the brain when we try and focus?

While your brain is focussing now as you read this book, there are at least three different types of attention enabling you to focus and concentrate:

1. **Selective attention** for focussing on one thing while disregarding others.
2. **Divided attention**, also known as 'attention switching', for managing and processing multiple sources of information at the same time. Driving a car is a good example — your attention needs to toggle back and forth almost continually.

3. **Sustained attention** for staying focussed on something for a long time. Your brain sorts and routes information so you can focus amid all the distractions and input that bombard you every day. It uses **sensitivity enhancement** to turn up or tune into sensory information like sounds and lights that can help process input more efficiently. Your brain focusses by filtering important information and moving it up the ladder for deeper processing while suppressing interruptions from irrelevant bits and pieces — a function known as **efficient selection.**

Your frontal cortex, which is responsible for resisting distractions and controlling our natural impulse to do something more fun, is hard at work when we are trying to keep our focus and attention on what we have chosen. Keeping this part of the brain running effectively requires a lot of energy, more than the parts of the brain that are active when we are thinking about nothing in particular. So, inevitably, at some point during the day, we run out of steam and that's when we might become distracted.

Once a distraction penetrates your focus it's hard to stop yourself from investigating further because your attention has already shifted. Now, the distraction becomes your focus and whatever you were focussing on begins to fade to the background.

DOES GETTING OLDER BLUR YOUR FOCUS?

Between the age of 40 and 60, the areas of the brain that suppress distractions may slow down so you can find it harder to ignore distractions or irrelevant information. It will differ depending on who you are, a lot of recent scientific studies looked at the effects of lifestyle on brain function; an active lifestyle helps keep your brain healthy, and exercise is particularly good for the brain.

THE BRAINWAVES OF FOCUS

We know that the most common brainwave state in adulthood is Beta, we stretch into Gamma which is the heightened super focussed state found in peak performance, but most of the time we are in Beta, the brainwaves of focus and attention, with the ability to switch between points of focus.

As we know, in childhood we are more in the Alpha and Theta states which are calmer, and more open to creativity and flow.

THE CURSE OF THE ABILITY TO MULTITASK

Multitasking has become second nature to many of us. We might be folding the laundry whilst listening to a podcast. Doing our online food shop whilst on a phone call with a work colleague or making a cup of coffee whilst reading this book. But how does this multitasking approach to life affect our ability to function and is it really possible to do more than one thing at a time, properly at least?

Research shows that when we multitask it changes the way the brain works. When we focus it activates the prefrontal cortex at the front of the brain, and both sides of the prefrontal cortex work in tandem. But when you multitask the two sides attempt to work independently, even though you think you are doing two things at once, in actual fact you are switching between these two sides. Although the switch takes a fraction of a second, those microseconds add up and it might take you up to 40 per cent longer to complete the same tasks than if you were to tackle them separately.[5]

Not only that, switching between tasks drains your cognitive resources making you more prone to making mistakes. Think of it like your phone battery, the more apps you have open, the more you use it, the more you drain the battery and eventually it needs to be recharged.

That said, more difficult tasks drain your battery or brain resources more than simple ones. So, you might find that folding the laundry and listening to a podcast feels as if you are completing both tasks well, whereas a difficult phone call whilst driving somewhere unfamiliar, would be trickier.

Distractions use up our attention span and prevent us from moving into deeper thought processes. Multitasking has other negative effects too; it affects your short-term memory and increases the stress hormones adrenaline and cortisol within the body. The trouble is, your prefrontal cortex craves new, novelty and the interesting. That's why we head for the easiest items on the to-do list rather than a longer, more complex task. Our brain loves the thrill of the win, every time we tick something off the list, we get a shot of hormones to the pleasure centre of the brain which can become addictive.[6]

Sophie Leroy,[7] a professor at the University of Minnesota says when we multitask we leave what is called an attention residue which is what we carry over from one task to another, where we're still thinking of a previous project as we start another. One analogy of this would be minimising a computer application, rather than closing it before opening another. The app is still running in the background, eating up the computer's processing power, diverting resources away from the current task.

Her study shows that 'people need to stop thinking about one task in order to fully transition their attention and perform well on another. Yet, results indicate it is difficult for people to transition their attention away from an unfinished task and their subsequent task performance suffers.'

In his book Deep Work,[8] Cal Newport suggests focussing on a single task for a long period of uninterrupted time to reach peak productivity. By ensuring the time block is truly uninterrupted (all notifications turned off, and mobile phone in another room) you don't get attention-residue issues. Cal suggests a four-hour block of time is a good place to start, maintaining intense focus any longer than this can prove difficult, but of course, it does depend on the individual and the task at hand. If there's one thing you should take away from this it's this: If possible, don't stop — or begin something else — until you're finished.

The danger with the rise of multitasking is that we have brought this into all areas of our life. How many times have you been watching a TV series or movie and midway through you have looked up the Wikipedia page of an actor or actress or historical event which was just mentioned? And that's the danger of distraction and the temptation of multitasking within the WOW framework, if we are distracted, we are not focussed and present and not able to fully immerse ourselves in the moment.

Children are not built to multitask, they are fully immersed and focussed on one thing. As adults we might try and encourage them to get on the multitasking bandwagon, as it is a more efficient use of our time. But this should be avoided at all costs.

THE MODERN WORLD IS SET UP FOR DISTRACTION

Cal Newport talks about the ability to focus in a modern, noisy, busy world. He describes modern working conditions as a killer of focus; open plan offices, instant messaging and the push for employees to be present on social media.

15 WAYS TO FIND FOCUS

We might think we know how to have a more focussed mind, but in fact a lot of what we think might help, goes against how the brain actually works. For example, there are many things that children do naturally, and researchers have found improves our focus, which might be counter-intuitive to what we would naturally do.

1. **Zoning out, allow your mind to wander and daydream.** Some psychologists believe that up to 50 per cent of our time we are in a daydreaming state, leading some researchers to argue that this is not laziness or a mind glitch, instead it is an essential feature which enables our brain to function.

We might think we have become distracted because our mind has wandered, but this dreaminess is likely a result of our nervous system doing necessary work of processing, reconfiguring, losing touch and then reconnecting.

Tip: If you have something you need to focus on, schedule in some daydreaming time, for example on your commute, so that this part of your brain has had its fix, and you don't become tempted to daydream when you actually need to focus on something.

Paul Seli, a psychologist at Harvard University, has distinguished between deliberate and accidental mind wandering, and says that only the accidental kind is bad for getting stuff done.[9] People who slot in their daydreaming when they know that it won't matter (when doing mindless admin, for example) suffer less than those whose minds skip off in a more uncontrolled manner.

'If the task is easy, intentional mind wandering will likely not result in performance costs, but it should afford people the opportunity to reap the benefits of mind wandering, such as problem-solving and planning,' he says.

Therefore, letting your mind off the hook now and again

might pay dividends. Giving yourself permission to think about anything but work not only takes the guilt out of mind wandering, but it might also help problem solve and ctrl-alt-del the mind too.

2. **Have fun and be playful, muck about.** Another thing that children are pretty good at. The rise of 'funny cat videos' online, and other forms of entertainment is a procrastinator's dream, and I am sure we all have times where we have been tempted to distraction by some amusing video a friend has sent us, and before we know it we are down a rabbit hole of (more or less) humorous content.

But there's good news cat fans, psychologists have found that having entertainment peppered throughout your day might actually put you in a better mental state for focus when you come back to the task in hand. Laughing improves willpower and energises the body and mind.

According to a recent study,[10] a good way to boost your reserves of willpower is to laugh. In experiments, people who had watched a funny video tried longer and harder to complete an impossible puzzle than a control group of people who watched a video that was relaxing but not funny. The study concluded that humour replenishes our reserves so effectively that workplaces should encourage a more 'playful' culture. 'Creating a culture of fun in your team – where you deliberately find something funny to laugh at, like a funny email or YouTube video would be one way of helping you to boost your work productivity. Of course, this isn't a blank cheque to watch cat videos all day but taking the occasional break to joke around is useful, especially when you are feeling really tired.'

3. **Make it harder to do your work.** You might think that you need to have clean and tidy, minimalist conditions with limited external distractions around you to be able to focus well, but perhaps you are wrong. Have you ever seen the desk of an artist or writer? Most of the ones I have seen are cluttered and piled high with notes and books and work. Which sounds very much like most children's bedrooms I see too.

I once saw a photograph of fashion designer Paul Smith's 'Creativity room' where he loves to work and create. Far from it being a minimalist white space, it is jam-packed with artefacts and objects from which he can draw inspiration for his projects. 'My room and all the objects in it are childlike not childish; the difference is huge. Children are not cluttered with education and experience, which makes them really open and honest. Some people might see it as junk; I see it as inspiration. Whether you work in a studio or a kitchen, it's the place you spend the most time thinking and creating. Having a few interesting objects around can help spark curiosity at just the right moment.'[11]

Nilli Lavie, a psychologist at University College London, came up with what she calls 'Load Theory'.[12] The idea is that there is a limit to how much information from the outside world our brains can process at any one time

– once all these processing 'slots' have been filled, the brain's attention system kicks in to decide what to focus on. Lavie's experiments suggest we might be better to work not in clean, tidy and silent surroundings, but in those that are messy and confusing. It works because once all the perceptual slots have been taken up, the brain must pour all its energies into focussing on the most important task. Distractions simply get screened out.

4. **Stop working.** When we are at school, we are forced to take regular breaks, at playtime and lunchtime, we are pushed outside in all winds and weathers to play games, and to take a strict and regimented lunchbreak (where the dinner supervisors are in charge) every single day. Children in the school system know that they need to take a break, and on more than one occasion I have heard cheers when the bell rings for playtime. As adults we sometimes forget this. We need to take breaks; our body and our mind needs them, our creativity needs them, and our focus and attention needs them. When you are on deadline, especially if you are in the flow state, taking a break might be the last thing on your mind, but you really must.

Some studies[13] suggest that due to natural variations in our cycle of alertness, we can concentrate for no longer than 90 minutes before needing a 15-minute break.

Other studies[14] have found that even a micro-break of a few seconds will work, provided it is a total distraction – in the studies, people did a few seconds of mental arithmetic, so you may have to do something more intense than staring out of the window.

Tip: Some form of exercise is a good thing to do in your break, as this energises and revs up the brain,[15] putting it into a better state to knuckle back down. Taking your exercise outdoors gives you a further boost – spending time in nature[16] has long been suspected to improve people's ability to focus. Meditation is another option. There is growing evidence that experienced meditators have better control over their attention[17] resources than non-meditators and are much better at noticing when it's time for a break. If that all sounds a bit time-consuming, the good news is that a quick dose of caffeine improves memory, reaction time and attention[18] in the short term.

5. **Less is more.** You need to pace yourself; it is impossible to completely focus for long periods and according to some studies, less is more.[19] Studies found that the most successful strategy was to focus for a while, and then to take a short break before going back to concentrating. People who tried to be 'on' all the time made more mistakes overall. Similarly, some research[20] found that people's attention resources stretched a little bit further when they were simply told to back off and think about something else instead of concentrating fully.

6. **Know what works for you, do not look for perfection – you are a human.** Writers know this well, and some of them develop routines to control their environment: They write with the same pen, at the same place, at the same hour of the day, while drinking the same drink and listening to the same music. Know your body clock. I, for one, am much more efficient in the morning, so I make sure to spend my first few hours on focussed work. Others suggest ignoring routines altogether. EB White, the author of Stuart Little and writer on The New Yorker says, 'A writer who waits for ideal conditions under which to work will die without putting a word on paper.'

The key is to give your mind just enough to do, so that your brain doesn't have the chance to look elsewhere for stimulation. For most people it might be a case of trial and error to find what works for them, but since screening out distractions can be tiring, perhaps this is one to use sparingly, when all else has failed. Finding the right kind of distraction and keeping it on the right side of being overwhelming can be tricky. There are a few apps that add visual or musical distractions to order, but so far none have been tested in scientific studies and may be no better than putting on the radio or a white noise soundtrack on in the background.

7. **Planning.** This helps with building resilience to interruptions and increases the ability to deal with challenges and setbacks.[21] It keeps us on course towards bigger goals and helps us meet life's difficulties head-on.

8. **Stay in one place and work on one thing at a time.** If you can remain focussed and stay in one setting, you are more likely to remain focussed. If interruptions do arise, it's easier to put aside what you are doing, and pick it up later.

9. **Rewards.** When we are in flow, it can be described as an autotelic experience, which means the experience is a reward in itself. If you are trying to focus on a goal you want to achieve, breaking down large projects into more manageable bits means we are rewarded more often. Researchers found that immediate rewards predicted whether or not someone would achieve their goals.[22] For example, when someone exercises to be healthier, we can tell if they will stick to their routine by simply looking at whether or not they're having a good time in their classes.

10. **Allow yourself to access the Flow state.** Flow is incredibly important in the WOW framework. I have already mentioned how entering the flow state, can help improve your focus and attention as well as all the other benefits it brings. To enter the flow state, Csikszentmihalyi recommends choosing a task that is challenging, but not overwhelming, removing distractions and being open to the experience. Accept the fact that progress is unpredictable, and let it happen naturally and just go with the flow.

11. **Examine the relationship with your phone.** One easy way to improve your focus is to look at your relationship with your phone and other devices. Check how many

notifications you allow. Monitor and regulate your screen time, utilise the 'focus' and productivity settings if you have them. Maybe use apps to help you with time management and workflow if that helps. One study showed that overindulging in social media and online surfing can be worse than losing a night's sleep, or even smoking marijuana.

Our 'always on' culture means that we are contactable and therefore distractable 24 hours a day unless we set some boundaries in place to protect our focus. Despite how often we are encouraged to 'unplug' from our devices, so many of us find it difficult to navigate. We have to remember that the algorithms of the internet and social media have been designed by armies of software engineers, statisticians and psychologists. What's incredible is that now we need our phones to rescue us from our phones with the global mindfulness meditation apps market size expected to reach over $4.2bn by 2027.[23]

12. **Breathe.** Pay attention to your breath, and where on your body you feel it most: direct your focus like a beam of light. Do this for three minutes a day, for a week and see how you feel.

13. **Practise.** It is becoming increasingly difficult to remain focussed with all the distractions around us. However, through practising simple mindfulness and focus-improving techniques such as labelling and flashlight we can develop the areas of the brain we use when in a focussed state. We can integrate these practices into everyday life, for

example using the flashlight technique when you are brushing your teeth. If your mind wanders and starts to think about your to-do list as you're brushing, bring the flashlight back, be mindful and focus on the sensations.

14. **Mindfulness, but remember the myths.** You are not 'clearing your mind.' This is an active mental workout. There is no 'blissed-out' state you are aiming to experience; in fact, the whole point is to be more present in the moment.

15. **Limit distractions and find your distraction limit.** Some focus best with silence, others need white noise in their headphones, while other people prefer loud rock music. Ultimately, the best approach depends on what works for you. We have learnt that distraction is inevitable. We can train the brain to improve our focus, and we can learn techniques to deal with and respond to distractions when they arise, which mean we don't fall down the rabbit hole of cat videos, never to return.

Losing FOCUS is one of the two main killers of WOW. When we become distracted, we freefall out of our desired states of NOW and FLOW, which bring us to WOW. Only when we are truly present, with a dedicated focus and attention, are we able to experience WOW.

'The truth is that you are living in a system that is pouring acid on your attention every day, then you are being told to blame yourself and to fiddle with your own habits while the world's attention burns.'[24]

– Johann Hari

'The key to happiness wasn't being yourself, because what did that even mean? Everyone had many selves. No. The key to happiness is finding the lie that suits you best.'

– Matt Haig

Chapter 11.

The killers of WOW: EGO

In this chapter we will look at the second of the two main killers of WOW, EGO. We will explore what we mean by the word ego in this sense, what exactly is your ego, how it develops over time, why is it such a villain when it comes to the WOW framework and what we can do to be aware of it and keep it in check.

The word 'Ego' often gets a bad press, so I think it's useful in the first instance to be clear about what I mean when I say your ego is likely to be one of the main WOW killers.

The word 'Ego' in Greek or Latin means 'I' and Ego has several definitions in our modern English language; it can mean a person's self-esteem (he needed an ego boost), it can refer to the part of the mind that meditates between conscious and unconscious and it can mean a sense of personal identity.

Although the word 'Ego' is often confused with vanity, and has other negative connotations, strictly speaking ego is a psychological term. Popularised by the founder of psychoanalysis, Sigmund Freud, it means the conscious mind or the awareness of one's own identity, self and existence.

And it is with this meaning we will be using the word for Find Your WOW.

You will have seen the word pop up already throughout this book, when we are talking about mindfulness and the separation of the ego or practising 'without judgement'. In the FLOW chapter, Mihaly Csikszentmihalyi describes the 'negation of the self' when we are in the flow state.

According to Freud's personality (psychoanalytic) theory,[1] the ego is one of the three parts which make up the human psyche: the id, the ego and the superego. Each of the three parts develop at different stages of our life.

The id is a part of the unconscious and responds only to what Freud called the pleasure principle (if it feels good, do it). As a new-born child we are completely id and only in later life do we develop an ego and superego. Even when we move into adulthood our id remains infantile, and is not changed by life, it operates only in the unconscious part of the mind. The id thinking is primitive, illogical, irrational with no concept of reality, it is selfish and pleasure driven.

'The ego is the only part of the conscious personality. It's what the person is aware of when they think about themselves and is what they usually try to project toward others.'

– Sigmund Freud

According to Freud, the ego part of our personality starts to develop around the age of two and is thought to be fully developed around eight years old. The ego moves between the unrealistic, selfish and pleasure-driven id, and the external real world. It works by using reason, realism, making decisions based on its view of the self and the personality and the role it plays within the external world. Ego considers etiquette, social norms and rules when it considers how to behave.

For ego, pleasure is sought through pain reduction or avoidance and its aim is to obtain pleasure through realistic means. Freud describes the analogy of the id being the horse and the ego is the rider. 'The ego is like a man on horseback, who has to hold in check the superior strength of the horse.' If the ego fails and anxiety is then experienced, our 'unconscious defence mechanisms' are employed to make us feel better.

Lastly, we move to the superego, which starts to develop around the age of five and incorporates the morals and values of society which are often learned from our parents and surrounding role models. The superego is the purveyor of rewards (pride and satisfaction) and punishments (shame and guilt). Superego is unconscious and is often said to be your inner voice, of conscience and self-criticism. Importantly, the superego consists of the conscience and the ideal self. It can punish the ego through guilt.

Freud also talks about the ego-ideal or the ideal self – an imaginary picture of how you 'ought' to be. It is thought that the ideal self and your conscience are largely determined in childhood from your parental values and how you were raised.

Carl Gustav Jung was a Swiss psychiatrist and psychoanalyst, and founder of analytical psychology.[2] He was contemporary to Freud and his personality hypothesis also involved the unification of consciousness and unconsciousness in a person. Jung viewed the ego as the centre of consciousness, while the self is the centre of the total personality, including consciousness, the unconscious and the ego.

Therefore, all of us have these three parts to our personality, with the ego the only conscious part, travelling between subconscious id and the superego. Why am I telling you this? Here are some thoughts:

1. We all have an ego, a sense of self which is a true version of who we are (held in our conscious)

2. We also have what is called a superego, which is an ideal version of yourself, an imaginary picture, and we often compare our true self to

3. As we grow older, we have more memories, experiences and social conformities to compare ourselves to, which could lead to conflict and tension between our ego (true self) and the primitive id and superego

4. Having an awareness of how you are behaving, your triggers and responses, is important in managing your personality, and mindfulness is one technique which can help with this

5. Listening to your inner voice can be damaging to your emotional health and well-being as well as your creativity, ambition and productivity

As you know, this book all started with me teaching meditation to over 15,000 children. I observed their natural mindfulness and flow ability, as well as their incredible curiosity of the world, leading me to the concept of WOW. One of the key observations for me (which has since been backed by research) was that the very youngest children had an underdeveloped ego. They were still learning about who they were and their place in the world, and at that point they were open to any possibilities. Ask any child what they would like to do for a job when they are older, and their responses are often full of big ambition. Until around that golden age of eight, they are often lacking in self-awareness, full of hopes and dreams for the future and prepared to give anything a go.

After this age, things begin to change.

They begin to see how they fit alongside the other personalities in the class, perhaps their character strengths and weaknesses. They are more self aware, not wanting to embarrass themselves in front of their friends or be laughed at or judged by others.

The greatest illustration I have for this is I often asked the children in my class questions, to which they would put their hands up for me to ask them to answer. In the first three or four years of primary school, up until the children are around eight or nine, the hands would shoot up before I had even finished asking the question. By the end of primary school, in the classes with the oldest children, I would be lucky if one or two hands would go up from a class of 30, and it would normally be the same children's hands who would be raised.

Without making this into a book on child development, I think it's useful to understand just a little more about what we are dealing with, the ego.

Scientists have found that there are set phases we travel through in childhood in order to develop our sense of self. Philippe Rochat created his Five Stages of Self Awareness[3] which describe how from birth until age five children learn to identify themselves, using a mirror test. The assessment became the leading authority on the subject. In essence, Level 1 'That's a mirror', Level 2 'There's a person in it', Level 3 'That person is me', Level 4 'That person is going to be me forever' and finally, Level 5, 'And everyone else can see it too'.

By the time children start school they are beginning to have a developed sense of self, but still an underdeveloped ego, as we have in adulthood. As we grow older, our ego grows in strength.

Therapists measure our ego strength because it is an excellent marker for overall mental health. It refers to our confidence and resilience in the face of stress, conflict or other challenges. It is also used as a sign of maturity and development.

You might think that when you are born you have a quiet ego, but no. At first your ego is 'noisy', egocentric and clamouring for selfish needs in the immediate moment. Eventually, the ego matures, and one learns to move beyond self-interest, to start to think from other people's points of view; to relate present actions to future outcomes; and to identify with people and experiences in an increasingly broader, deeper manner. Furthermore, many qualities of the noisy ego are hallmarks of relative immaturity, whereas many qualities of the quieter ego characterise psycho-social maturity.[4]

Studies[5] have concluded that while ego increases with age until adolescence, it levels off quickly in early adulthood, with most adults ceasing to mature beyond the self-aware stage. Research has found that around middle age, there is no longer a growth in our ego.[6]

Furthermore, Robert Kegan's Adult Development Theory highlights five distinct developmental stages, where becoming an 'adult' involves transitioning to higher stages of development. Ultimately, this means developing an independent sense of self and gaining the traits associated with increasing social maturity.[7]

In some spiritual practices such as Buddhism, eliminating suffering through conquering the ego and embracing our true self is a central goal.

Eckhart Tolle brilliantly describes ego in his book, A New Earth[8:] 'An ego that wants something from another – and what ego doesn't – will usually play some role to get its "needs" met, be they material gain, a sense of power, superiority, or specialness, or some kind of gratification, be it physical or psychological. Usually, people are completely unaware of the roles they play. Some roles are subtle; others are blatantly obvious, except to the person playing it. Some roles are designed simply to get attention from others. The ego thrives on others' attention, such as recognition, praise, admiration, or just to be noticed in some way, to have its existence acknowledged.'

So, when you are considering how your ego might impact your enjoyment and experience of WOW, it's worth considering some of the roles you might play in your everyday life and how those roles affect your true self.

For instance, when our children misbehave[9] we might react badly because it challenges our idea of ourselves as good parents. We can instead choose not to take our kids' choices personally, and recognise that they are developing into their own separate individuals.

Someone who identifies with a certain position or amount of wealth might spiral into depression when they suffer a financial setback, or lose a job.[10] When instead they can recognise that the loss is painful, but that they are not any less valuable or worthy because of it.

HERE ARE 15 WAYS TO TAME YOUR EGO
1. **Check in and have awareness**
Drawing our minds back to the present moment each time our thoughts threaten to slip into the past or run ahead to the future is a powerful tool. Being present in the now keeps us from becoming overwhelmed by our ego's relentless demands. Also notice what triggers your ego.

2. **Be happy with what you've got – Be grateful and practise gratitude**
Our ego is always hustling for more, so many of us walk

around with vague feelings that we don't measure up no matter what we do. Ego loves to tell us that we are not good enough. So, gratitude is another powerful tool we can use. When we begin to feel as if we're missing out or failing to measure up, we can take a moment to express our gratitude for what already is.

3. **Don't compare yourself to others**
It's increasingly difficult in an age of social media but try not to compare your life to the filtered lives of others, especially online. Our ego is never satisfied with what we already have and causes us to become anxious or even depressed when we aren't actively working toward the next accomplishment, goal, relationship or other object of desire. So, we keep working, keep accumulating, keep striving, while our planet, relationships and bodies pay the price.

4. **Celebrate your individuality and imperfections**
Wabi-sabi is a Japanese concept centred on the idea of accepting imperfection. It focusses on highlighting the beauty that is simple and imperfect, for example concentrating on the simplicity and the harmony that is found in natural elements. At the end of the day, we are all perfectly imperfect.

5. **Practice mindfulness**
Our ego doesn't like the present moment. In fact, awareness of the present moment is the death of ego. Our ego is at play when we are wrapped up in thoughts about the past or we

are fixated on the future; the next promotion, whether we will pass that test, the dream house or retirement. Mindfulness meditation makes us more aware of the present moment and the thoughts that enter our minds. It also helps us to slow down and pay better attention to our lives, become more aware of the roles we've learned to play and decide if we want to play them.

6. **Loving kindness**
Ego wants us to feel superior to other people. As you start to grow more aware of your own ego, you'll most likely begin to recognise it at play in other people and start to feel a little smug. Instead of forcing enlightenment on others, exercise patience and kindness, remembering that everyone else is on the same journey and that is their path not yours.

7. **Be honest with yourself and resist defending your ego**
Our ego does not respond well to criticism and will react by becoming defensive or accusatory. This only further strengthens the ego and hampers our personal growth. Instead, resist the urge to jump to our own defence right away, and instead simply absorb and consider the criticism. That way when we do finally react it comes from a place of awareness, and not ego.

8. **Practice curiosity**

When our ego is triggered, instead of berating ourselves for not being mindful or more mature, we can embrace curiosity. Almost in a childlike way. It's difficult at first to become curious in the moment. With practice, we can look back on our worst reactive moments. Only when we can uncover the root of our reactions will we see real change.

9. **Look at the bigger picture**

If you can consider that you are one part of something bigger, it can help to tame your ego.

10. **Make mistakes on purpose**

The ego craves perfection and if you create opportunities to experiment, create and make mistakes, this will mean there is imperfection which necessarily will tame your ego.

11. **Admit when you are wrong**

Along the lines of the previous point, admitting when you are wrong, acknowledging any lessons you have learnt and mistakes that you have made and move on, ego in check.

12. **Compliment and praise others**

If you consider the talent, brilliance and efforts of others it is not only a kind thing to do, but it also tames the ego.

13. **Work on self-improvement**
Recognising that you don't know everything, and have room for improvement and development is a great way to tame the ego.

14. **Draw a web of connections, consider the butterfly or ripple effect**
Think about how the world is interconnected and the small, but significant part you play. It helps to get some sense of perspective and quietens the ego.

15. **Flow!**
Finding ways and experiences where you can access flow will mean that your ego will be quietened and tamed.

12 MANTRAS FOR LETTING GO OF YOUR EGO
- It's not all about you
- Just do it
- Get over yourself
- No one cares
- The key to getting unstuck is to know where the block really exists
- Your ego is yours to shape and mould. Be bold with the design
- Take back the power and actually do something
- The true purpose of your ego is to show you what matters
- Let go
- What is the worst that can happen?
- Nothing in life is perfect
- That's their path not yours, stick to your own

WHERE IS MY EGO?

Almost 100 years ago, a little-known (but fascinating) neuroscientist called Constantin von Economo played a huge part in discovering where we believe the ego lies, when he peered down his microscope and saw a handful of brain cells that were long, spindly and much larger than the others. At first, he thought they were a sign of disease, but the more brains he looked at, the more of these peculiar cells he found and always in the same two small areas which had evolved to process smells and flavours.[11]

After decades more research, we now call these neurons VENs (Von Economo Neurons), named after Constantin himself. Scientists believe that VENs give us our sense of 'I' and empathy, as well as organise and monitor other parts of the brain.[12]

To put it simply, these neurons (of which there are just a few hundred thousand in numbers) are like an orchestra conductor who directs our thoughts and helps us in our concentration, and it is thought that the VENG (von Economo Neuron Group) could be the initiator and home of our ego. The VENG and brain signals control each other to form a stable ego. When there is a mismatch, then either the ego gets inflated leading to conflict or gets deflated leading to depression and low self-esteem. Similarly, when we do not get what we want, or we fail at something (again a conflict between our ego and reality) we get angry or frustrated. The VENG makes it possible to initiate conflict resolution, which is an important aspect of an evolved human being and comes from having a calm mind and the benefit of wisdom and experience.

Incredibly, our VENs start forming just after birth, and reach their maximum number of 200,000–400,000, by the age of eight. This is also the age by which a sense of self is ingrained as a brain map. Therefore, before the age of eight we have an underdeveloped sense of self, which means our inner conscience and critic is not as vocal as it is in adulthood.

Linking in with the earlier chapter on why children are the masters of WOW, we can see that in a child's brain development this inner critic or analytical brain doesn't happen until the late Alpha years, as they tiptoe into the Beta phase of adulthood. Children of around ten onwards will noticeably start to be more self-aware, self-deprecating, self-conscious. If we can just stay in the flow state where the inner critic is silenced as we can be our 'Self', then we will be on the road to WOW.

The joy of childhood is that we have not yet encountered the obsession with self and ego, a fear of failure, a comparison with others, a sense of our role in society, the pressure of social norms, the pressure to conform and burden of being pigeonholed. As a child we are free to learn, to think, to play, to feel, to flow, to be present. A perfect breeding ground for mindfulness. Later in life our ego and sense of self can get in the way to achieving mindfulness, flow and experience WOW.

As children grow and develop, from the age of eight and beyond into the tween and teenage years, they start to become more self-aware, self-obsessed and self-conscious. The introduction of the online world as a point of reference, the importance of social media, and a culture and climate of instant gratification, praise and rewards means that the childhood psyche is altered.

The negation of the self or the quietening of the inner critic, is an important aspect of mindfulness, but also one of the key conditions required for flow. According to the principles of psychologist Mihaly Csikszentmihalyi which identified the conditions required for the flow state, when people are experiencing flow, they are so involved in an activity that nothing else seems to matter. This is how people in flow can find pleasure in whatever they are doing; work, relationships, hobbies and experiences. Whatever you are doing, you are doing it for the pleasure of the experience itself rather than any reward, award or gratification.

To access flow, we also need to release a sense or burden of the 'self' and value being and remaining in the present moment, as we do in childhood. This is the foundation on which Carl Jung coined 'Calling upon your inner child.' He linked this internal child archetype to past experiences and memories of innocence, playfulness, and creativity, along with hope for the future. The 'inner child' concept has been developed further in popular psychology as a subconscious mindset or unconscious subpersonality which is built from what a person learns and experiences in the earliest years but influences the mind later in life.

Blindekuh is a restaurant in Basel, Switzerland, where you

enjoy your meals completely in the dark, and the waiting staff are blind. I once went for a meal and was blown away by the experience. Having to find new and innovative ways to cut my food, pour the wine and find my way around the restaurant. If you hear sounds around you, you are not 100 per cent sure from which direction they came, and the darkness somehow does something to the whole taste sensation. Without being able to see what you are eating is an incredible experience which of course people with sight difficulties or blindness are faced with every day. During Covid many people reported losing their sense of taste and smell, which meant their sensory enjoyment, fulfilment and satisfaction of say, culinary experiences of WOW were altered. I have had tinnitus since I was around eight or nine years old, so my life has a high-pitched ringing soundtrack of varying intensity, so much so now almost 40 years on, I hardly seem to notice it. Finding WOW is a unique and personal experience and this is even more true when you either temporarily or permanently have a disability of some sort.

One area where I have noticed a difference in the sense of self or ego is when running Creative Play sessions. On a few occasions I have left a blank piece of paper on a table in front of children, and indeed in a corporate setting. I have asked them (both children and the adults) to work in pairs to sketch a portrait of their partner.

After a few giggles, children get to work with barely a moment to spare. The adults on the other hand, often look horrified as if I am the cruellest person in the world, to make them do something like this, something so childlike and belittling, something so out of their comfort zone. Maybe you have been in this situation. For many of the grown-ups they are looking around the room to see how their colleagues are approaching the task, making a mark on a page then screwing it up into a ball before taking another piece of paper. Remarks of 'I can't do this' and 'this is impossible' sing around the room. But eventually they might just have a go. What happens between this time of childhood and unbound creativity, and have a go attitude, to the rabbit-in-the-headlights atmosphere of the corporate boardroom where there is fear of not doing it well enough, being laughed at or judged or failing in some way in the eyes of others, is quite remarkable.

Note: I occasionally also run Laughter Yoga sessions with similar results.

How many of you are parents with children who have brought home their 'artistic masterpieces' from school and want to display them around the home? A gallery of beautiful efforts and imperfection, creativity, play and experiments. To us they are beautiful works of art, pinned to the side of the fridge until the colours have faded, and the Christmas angel that was made when your child was five, and now aged 16 they say, 'oh mum, do you have to get it out again?'

Creativity and play are perfect hunting grounds where you can try and battle your ego to the ground. I promise you, when the ego is down on the ground, you are on your way to victory on the battlefield of WOW.

'Midlife is the time to let go of an over dominant ego and to contemplate the deeper significance of human existence.'

– Carl Gustav Jung

It is important to remember the three personality parts I mentioned at the top of the chapter are competing for your attention, and the only one in the conscious is your ego. It is the one you can nurture, get to know, have an awareness of and to a certain extent grow into what you want it to be.

When researching for this book, one of the common responses I received when asking midlifers about how they feel about their sense of self, was the feeling that 'I have lost myself.' The difficulty of retaining a sense of who we really are, our desires, our personalities, honouring our needs and interests, maintaining our boundaries, often becomes more difficult as we get older. Even the ability to carve out some 'me time' might become tricky and a rare treat rather than a regular occurrence. When we are having competing pressures and demands on our love, our time, our energy and our resources, it can be difficult to keep a sense of balance. We can become blinded by the roles we are being forced to be, especially in midlife where perhaps you are caring for children and older members of the family. Your work and professional life. Friends and social life. Looking after the health and well-being of yourself and those around you. Puberty of teens which coincides with the menopause of mums. Social media and screens. Retirement and redundancy. Trying to make the finances work. I could go on. If any of us can maintain a sense of who we truly are amongst all this, then I think we are doing pretty well.

'There comes a time when the only way to start living is to tell the truth. To be who you really are, even if it is dangerous.'

– Matt Haig

'Part of me suspects that I'm a loser, and the other part of me thinks I'm God Almighty.'

– John Lennon

'Life is a compromise of what your ego wants to do, what experience tells you to do, and what your nerves let you do.'

– Walter Bagehot

'Do one thing every day that scares you.'

– **Eleanor Roosevelt**

Chapter 12.

Other WOW killers

This is a short chapter to encourage you to give some thought to the other potential killers of WOW, these are both internal and external and to a certain extent within your control, and not.

1. **Time:** You will never experience moments of WOW if you do not stop, to be in the moment, or make time for the WOW to happen. You don't need to allow a huge amount of time. Also consider the pace at which you live your life. If you are always rushing from place to place, you might think you are allowing the time for WOW, but, you are only experiencing a tiny fraction of what that WOW could be and the impact it could have. But, that said, any WOW is better than no WOW at all.

2. **Mindset:** As we will explore in The new WOW order chapter, there are ten principles of the WOW mindset to consider. Arguably, one of the most important of these is a mindset of permission, you need to give yourself permission to experience WOW; let go of the ego, let go of the guilt and the temptation to rush or become distracted. Other key aspects of the overarching mindset is to approach

everything as if it is brand new, with awareness, curiosity and intrigue.

3. **People:** As we know, being around and spending time with the 'right' people can magnify, extend and deepen the impact of the WOW experience. You will also get to know your fellow WOW warriors (whether you choose to tell them this or not). These are the people that often by merely being in their company will force you to have moments of WOW. However, you will also need to get to know your WOW drainers too who perhaps have a different type of energy and perhaps manage to kill any WOW experience.

4. **Access:** You might be thinking that where you live, or your access to certain facilities or opportunities might be a killer of WOW, and this might be true if you have a specific experience in mind. However, as you will see more from 6) and 7) below, there is WOW all around us. Wherever you live, whoever you are, you just have to hunt it down and find it.

5. **Boundaries:** We all have boundaries in place to protect ourselves from getting hurt or from feeling uncomfortable in certain situations, whether we choose to articulate these or not. These are personal and entirely fixed by you. They might, quite rightly, be a killer of WOW, and that is completely fine. You should never feel pressure to do anything you do not want to do.

6. **Money:** They say the best things in life are free, and as I grow older, I tend to agree. My happiest moments are often

when I am experiencing the simple pleasures in life; with my loved ones, in nature, having fun and good times with friends. I really believe that the natural world offers the greatest opportunity for moments of WOW and it is where I have experienced the majority of mine. A close second, would be having WOW-inducing conversations with other people who I am somehow in awe of, and find truly inspirational. The place where I find my third most WOW-inducing moments are when eating and drinking, specifically when I can enjoy simple, beautifully cooked food. The first two of these needn't cost a penny and when I think of one of most mouth-watering food-related WOWs, it was a margherita pizza in a backstreet pizzeria in Turin. The pizza was made up of just four ingredients and cost four Euros, but man it was good.

7. **Unrealistic expectations:** In a world filled with social media and 'perfect' lifestyles, it can be hard to settle for a moment of WOW in your local park but remember what is at play here is your ego, and this as we know is one of the main two killers of WOW. If we don't have any expectation as to the frequency, quality or content of the WOW, this will add to the element of surprise. The important thing to remember is that we try to look at the world with new eyes, through the eyes of a child and with that, everything will be new and exciting. Happiness as we know is on the inside and not determined by any external source. If we can find joy and pleasure in the simple things in life, we can have a lifetime of happiness.

8. **Fear:** Fear might be a killer of WOW, which again is linked

to your ego. Everything I say here is with the presumption that you are acting in line with your boundaries. We need to remember that fear is a natural part of being a human being, it is what keeps us alive. But when fear cripples us and stops us trying new things, saying yes to opportunities and leaping into the unknown, fear might be a killer of WOW. Some WOW opportunities will come when we push ourselves to the edge of our comfort zone, just as Mihaly Csikszentmihalyi refers to in the flow state which occurs when our ability and challenge is perfectly matched, or rather slightly mismatched in that we feel pushed and challenged. So, if you can, be brave, what's the worst that can happen? You might just Find Your WOW at the other side of fear.

9. **The mundane:** Linked to fear is the desire to stay in your comfort zone, surrounded by routine and life admin. In the WOW-less world, we realise that as adults a lot of what we do is boring, mundane and the same. Of course, we can't always have a life of glitz, glamour and excitement, but we can look for the moments of WOW amongst the monotony. If we just accept that this is how our life has to be, it can become depressing and overwhelming. This is why the mundane can be a killer of WOW, but we have to push through and see the world in a fresh way, it's a world full of opportunities to experience WOW, even in the household chores, gardening and daily commute. You just need to find the WOW, it's there, it might be hidden, but it's there.

10. **Health:** We are all picking up this book at a different point and place in our life, with our own considerations around our physical, mental and emotional health. In partnership with the boundaries point above, it is important that we work with what we have, are able and comfortable to do.

One thing worth noting is that stress plays a huge role in how well we feel, with one in four adults in the UK with a mental health diagnosis.[1] As we have already explored in the book, your ability to find WOW might be determined by how you are feeling. Stress affects our motivation, our ability to focus, how we feel or regulate our emotions, our self-esteem, morale and our inclination to catastrophise and feel a lack of self-worth. Many others are struggling with loneliness, loss of connection to others and feeling like they have lost a sense of purpose.

So many of us have experienced mental health challenges at various points in life, I get it. As Charlie Mackesy wrote in The Boy, the Mole, the Fox and the Horse, 'If you can see the next step, take that.' For some people, it is about taking the baby steps towards WOW, you might choose to focus on one of the five pillars, even trying to work on the killers of WOW rather than aiming for the full framework, and that is just perfect. Do what you can, you're amazing.

'Life is not measured by the number of breaths we take, but the moments that take our breath away.'

– Anonymous

Chapter 13.

Good WOW hunting

Theory is one thing, now you need to decide to make time to Find Your WOW. These don't need to be rare and life-changing moments. WOW can be found all around us in our everyday lives.

'Awe. We talk about it as if it's a once-in-a-lifetime thing, but in fact it's everywhere.'

– Keltner

HOW OFTEN SHOULD YOU FIND YOUR WOW?
Of course, I am going to say you need to do this as often as possible, but we know how busy life can be. My advice is to try and diarise ten minutes of WOW per day (a window of wonder) or even a full hour per week where you can follow the five pillars and fully immerse yourself in a WOW-inducing activity. This might be a new experience or simply doing an everyday task more mindfully, with childlike eyes, with more awe and wonder.

By taking time to engineer more WOW into your day, you might rediscover things which bring you fulfilment, purpose and joy, and bring some of the benefits of mindfulness and flow to your health and well-being.

We are on the lookout for activities in our everyday which enable us to: Pause for a moment (be in the **NOW**), where you can **FOCUS** your attention on what you are doing, minimising distractions. Be fully absorbed in the task to try to access the state of **FLOW**, relax, don't let that **EGO** or inner critic get in the way, and finally, cultivate the right conditions to allow awe and wonder to creep in, expose yourself to vastness which challenges your way of thinking or view of the world and then, my friends, you will likely Find Your **WOW**.

Earlier I described the ten overarching principles for cultivating the conditions for WOW and just to remind you, here they are again:

1. Learning and discovery
2. Experimenting and failing
3. Creativity
4. Play
5. Using our senses
6. Out of comfort zone
7. Something new
8. New way of doing something old
9. Making time
10. Connectedness

Here are my 'quick WOW wins' which you can weave into your day, to feel the benefits of awe and wonder and Find Your WOW.

They can be summarised in the following categories; we will explore each of these in more detail and why they are so important to Find Your Wow.

1. Experiences in nature
2. Experiences with your WOW warriors
3. Experiences with a sense of history or that give you a sense of the vastness of space and time
4. Having the mindset of a tourist, even in places you have visited before
5. Using a WOW randomiser (more on this later)
6. Using technology to experience screen-based, digital and virtual WOWs
7. Read, listen, watch content which broadens your horizons and see the world from new perspectives
8. WOW 101, learn the basics of what is around you
9. WOW journeys; commutes, regular walks and trips
10. Being more childlike

Done regularly.

EXPERIENCES IN NATURE

'We all have a thirst for wonder. It's a deeply human quality. Science and religion are both bound up with it. What I'm saying is, you don't have to make stories up, you don't have to exaggerate. There's wonder and awe enough in the real world. Nature's a lot better at inventing wonders than we are.'

– Carl Sagan

Throughout the book, I have talked a lot about the important role nature plays in finding WOW in our life. If we think of our top ten WOW moments from our life, it is likely that nature played a part in a significant number of them, and this is backed by research. In one study participants were asked to recall a time they had encountered a 'really beautiful' natural scene and then rate the extent to which 'awe' described their experience on a 1 to 7 scale, the average rating for 'awe' was 6.[1]

When researching for this book, whenever I asked people to think of a recent time they have said WOW, I would say around eight times out of ten it would involve an experience which took place outdoors, where they were able to experience the wonder and beauty of nature.

Despite what one might expect, rarely this would be a 'grand' WOW of say, visiting the Great Barrier Reef or scaling a mountain. Often, it would be very 'normal' experiences which were in some way surprising or inspiring. For example, the first time they saw a wild pony on the moors, the time they found a fossil on a beach, that time a robin came up super close and they had a moment of connection.

During the pandemic, many of us became more appreciative of our natural world, the environment and wildlife in our local community. As we were not being able to travel and visit new places, we had to make the most of the outdoors on our doorstep. Many people said their daily walks were the highlight of their day, taking time outside, and enjoying simple activities with loved ones. Many of us might have vowed that we would keep doing this once we went 'back to normal', but how many of us have?

Being in nature is not only good for our physical and mental health, but it is also one of the main theatres of WOW. Nature presents a constant of change, unpredictability and imperfection. An ever-changing and evolving exhibition to visit, to discover and WOW over. Numerous studies have shown that spending time in nature lowers stress and improves our health by decreasing blood pressure, enhancing focus, and strengthening our immune system.

Experiencing awe and wonder is one of the main factors[2] that makes nature so powerful. Importantly, you don't need to visit the Grand Canyon or the Great Barrier Reef to get a dose of awe from nature.[3] 'It can just be a walk through a forest that's near your house', says Dr Jennifer Stellar.[4]

I have an allotment, and love to spend time there growing fruit, vegetables and flowers, it really is a perfect WOW activity.

When you think of moments of WOW, you might remember experiences from nature; a beautiful view, a buzzard soaring high above you, the power of a storm. But we now know even digital experiences of the natural world can give us a sense of awe. The King of Natural WOWs would have to be Sir David Attenborough, and any of the wonderful BBC Natural History Unit content (in particular, the 'Planet' series) would be enough to give you a quick WOW fix whenever you're most in need. These are available in short clips on YouTube if you do not have access to the BBC.

It is well documented that experiencing green spaces is good for our mental health. In fact, the latest studies have shown that when green and blue spaces collide, it has the greatest positive effect on the brain.[5]

Interestingly, researchers have discovered that experiencing the natural green and blue colours digitally via a screen can give us some of those all-important mental health benefits.

EXPERIENCES WITH WOW WARRIORS

Being around the right people, and perhaps more importantly avoiding spending too much time with the 'wrong' people can make or break your WOW experiences. Those people who inspire, connect and motivate you are your WOW warriors. Some of these people you will know, some of these people you have never met in your life, and possibly never will.

Of the ones you know, these are the people who share the same mindset and follow the pillars of WOW. These are the ones who will suggest you try that new restaurant in town, are up for crazy adventures, are spontaneous, the people who you most easily have fun and laugh with. They are perhaps the ones, that if you had known them in childhood, they would have been your closest friends. The ones which encourage, support and enthuse you. These are the people you are likely to have WOW experiences with.

The next set of WOW warriors you might or might not know, these are the people who make you say WOW because of what they do, who they are or the talents they have.

Being with, or learning about people with talent, who have achieved great things or shown incredible courage can inspire WOW. Hearing stories of individuals such as Anne Frank, Martin Luther King or Greta Thunberg can be awe-inspiring. Autobiographies are often a good place to start to find moments of WOW, but you could also try a podcast where you can listen to an interview with an inspirational person.

We can also experience moments of WOW when **observing someone with vast skills, talent or unique abilities**. Consider for a moment that there are 8 billion+ people on the planet who you could potentially connect with (and the fact that with the internet, you could connect with over 40 per cent of them from the comfort of your own home) is a real moment of WOW.

Coming back to your WOW warriors, we have explored that you might know them, you might not. They might be your companions to experience WOW with, they might inspire WOW in you because of what they do or say. But there is another crucial set of WOW warriors which you might not have considered.

Those people who share your passions, beliefs and goals. Simply being a part of a crowd of people can have a WOW effect. Several studies[6] have shown that when we move in unison with others, whether that is playing music in a band, dancing at a festival or cheering on a sports team, we can feel bonded to those around us and produce a state of flow.

Being in the company of someone with great talent can create that feeling of vastness and change of perspective associated with awe. That's why when you're listening to a singer hit the high notes or a musician perform an incredible solo you might feel emotional, get goosebumps or what people call 'the chills.'[7]

Some of the best WOW warriors, are children and young people who are, as we have discovered, more open to experiencing WOW through their mindset of curiosity, awe and wonder, creativity, fun and play. One of the best ways to engineer more WOW into your life is to spend time with young children; their world is new, vast and awe-inspiring. Time spent with especially little children is an immersion in WOW. If you don't have your own children, ask if you can hang out with younger members of your family or community or volunteer at a local group. Simply by being with them, you can't help but catch a bit of that childlike enthusiasm for yourself.

Being around children means we can start to see life with their eyes. The phrase we often hear is 'out of the mouths of babes' but maybe it should be 'through the eyes of babes'. Try to immerse yourself in their world a little, whenever you can. Asking them questions that maybe an eight-year-old version of you would ask, listen out for their own little WOWs, allow yourself some unbridled time to get creative and play with them. Use your imagination and see where it leads. I always say after a day of teaching in the classroom, that I am sure I have learnt as much if not more from the children, than the children have learnt from me.

'A child's world is fresh and new and beautiful, full of wonder and excitement. It is our misfortune that for most of us that clear-eyed vision, that true instinct for what is beautiful and awe-inspiring, is dimmed and even lost before we reach adulthood. If I had influence with the good fairy who is supposed to preside over the christening of all children, I should ask that her gift to each child in the world be a sense of wonder so indestructible that it would last throughout life, as an unfailing antidote against the boredom and disenchantment of later years … the alienation from the sources of our strength.'

– Rachel Carson[8]

You will find your fellow WOW warriors (whether you choose to tell them that is who they are to you or not). These are the people that often by merely being in their company will force you to have moments of WOW. You will also get to know your WOW drainers too, who perhaps have a different type of energy, but enough about them, and you know exactly who I am talking about.

Strangers can be WOW-inducing too, and for me stories are a big part of my life. As a journalist and from working in PR, a huge part of my life has involved story gathering, story receiving and storytelling. So much so that those three aspects make up a storytelling workshop which I have run in organisations all over the UK.

Being in the presence of someone you don't know well

(or even someone you do know well), can give you an opportunity to go WOW hunting. Imagine if you knew that everyone you will ever meet from this point on has a story which will enable you to have a moment of WOW, if only you can uncover it. What an amazing thought that is. And think of all the WOWs you can hunt down.

For six years, I worked as a reporter at the BBC. I was sent to remote parts of the East Midlands in England to try and unearth stories from the man or woman on the street; stories which hadn't come from a tip-off or press release. Stories and voices which unless I found them, would probably never be heard. This fired a real passion and sense of purpose within me. It was my job to find the stories that would make the radio listeners say WOW. They might be stopped in their tracks, and maybe the story would have a lasting effect on their life.

There was the man who had been stranded on a Japanese island during nuclear bomb testing, there was the woman who had bumped into a school friend in an art gallery in Australia after 50 years and they now spoke every week, there was the man who had learnt to walk again after a sledging accident in his childhood, there was a woman who painted incredible pictures but was completely blind.

Time after time, day after day, I thought my luck would run out and the stories would dry up and I would not be able to do my job. But then I realised something, which has remained true and with me to this day. Everyone has not only one, but countless stories, numerous ways to bring a moment of WOW. It just takes an investment of time, attention, curiosity, the flow of a conversation and 'active listening' to allow them to tell their story in their own way, without any judgement, and I promise, the WOW will come. One teacher once said to her class, quoting Epictetus, the Greek philosopher: 'You all have two ears and one mouth, which means each day you should listen for twice as long as you speak'.[9] I have always remembered this phrase and tried to honour it in conversations with the people I meet. And I am sure I have discovered more WOWs from other people, simply by following that ratio.

So, you see, you can Find Your WOW, vicariously through other people. Whether it is in conversation, or performance, in person or from a distance at a concert or via a screen.

Conversations are the most simple and easy way to experience WOW, and what's wonderful is that this can immediately become a part of your everyday life; with your work colleagues, friends and family or strangers. Of course, you might not feel comfortable sparking a conversation with people you have never met before, and you will set your own boundaries, but in everyday conversations, WOWs can be found. And crucially, it gives you an opportunity to practise your good WOW hunting, you never know where it might lead.

Experiences with a sense of history or that give you a sense of the vastness of space and time. Whether it is looking back over history or considering what might happen in the future, perhaps it is looking at your own ancestry that has led to you being here at this moment or considering the great expanse of universe beyond our own planet. Experiences which expand our horizons both literally and in our mind are very often also moments of WOW.

My son's fascination with dinosaurs has gone beyond his early childhood. Even now he is a teenager we love to research and explore the Dorset Jurassic coast near where we live. Going down to the beach after a storm to see if we can unearth a fossil is one of our favourite WOW-inducing experiences.

Being able to imagine prehistoric creatures walking, flying and swimming around the very place where we are standing is awesome. Similarly, visits to museums and historical places often help us to bring to mind people and creatures who were living hundreds or thousands of years before us. These experiences aren't just enjoyable and pleasurable, they in fact change and alter our perspective on things, how we view life and see ourselves as part of some larger story. They bring us WOW.

My son has a telescope, and we love to take it out onto the balcony at night to look at the moon, track satellites, space stations and identify planets and stars. If ever I need a quick WOW fix, this is my go-to solution. We have an app which, if we point it at the night sky, tells us what we can see, and gives us a bit more information, there's always a moment of WOW.

Take time to think about the vastness of the planet. Consider the size of the ocean. Much like the land's surface with mountains and hills, the ocean floor or seabed isn't completely flat. There are all sorts of underwater landforms such as canyons, trenches and underwater volcanoes.

Amazingly, the average depth of the ocean is 3,700 metres! Why not research some of the estimated 8.7 million species on earth, ranging from the smallest microorganism to a blue whale.

One ultimate awe experience might come from seeing Earth from space. A 2016[10] paper by the psychologist David Yaden includes several quotes from astronauts discussing this experience, sometimes called the 'overview effect'.[11] While most of us will never be able to truly experience this first-hand, you can still get a dose of awe from viewing the International Space Station's live feed of Earth.[12] In a similar vein, I use Chrome's Earth View from Google Earth browser extension,[13] which displays an image from across the globe each time I open a new tab. Yaden founded the Varieties Corpus, a website where people can share and learn about self-transcendent and awe-inspiring experiences.[14]

'We can't solve problems by using the same kind of thinking we used when we created them.'

– Albert Einstein

Having the mindset of a tourist, even to places you have been before. It can be difficult to feel a lot of awe towards the same sights you see every day, even if they are beautiful. But you don't have to go far to find something new.

One thing I love to do is become a tourist for the day in a place I have visited many times before, even my hometown.

With technology you can use online maps to search for new places to visit. My partner has a game where he gets into the car with his young son and allows him to say Left or Right at each junction for about 20–30 minutes to see where they end up. My son and I have tried the 'pin in a map' challenge where one of us wears a blindfold and pushing a pin into the map to decide where to go for a daytrip in the school holidays. (Or simply how about jumping on a city tour bus where you live?)

Using a WOW randomiser. Why not collect ideas for places you think you might be able to experience WOW, write them on pieces of paper, fold them up and put them in a glass jar. When you are feeling like you are lacking in a little WOW you can turn here for some inspiration.

Using technology to experience screen-based, digital WOWs. Although I have passionately argued that technology does not play a huge role in finding WOW, I am about to contradict myself slightly. Of course, tech can have negative connotations when it comes to killing our focus and flow, it can also be a place to find WOW, if used for good.

I love to run, and I use the running app Strava to check out new runs in my neighbourhood, it is also great to go on walks or runs throughout the different seasons as that will also bring some WOW to the same experience.

When you reach for the phone, rather than aimlessly scrolling social media, you could try and have a moment of WOW.

Some easy ideas are listening to sounds of nature on Spotify, or an inspirational podcast where you can expand your horizons and discover something new. Or perhaps trying to learn some words or phrases from a different language and celebrating when you've remembered them the next day. Reading an article about a subject that you know little about can begin to expand your views and change your perception of the world just a little.

One idea might be to have a **WOW folder** on your phone to save and capture some pictures and save them for a literal rainy day, a digital memory bank, where you make time to relive memories from WOW-inducing trips by looking at photographs and videos. These can also be lovely to share, by sending your WOW moments to others.

Virtual Reality (VR) presents an interesting opportunity to induce WOW because it can 'overcome our sense of physics and challenge our assumptions about the world'.[15] One study found that immersive videos, a highly realistic form of VR, that displayed 'vast and panoramic scenes of natural beauty from a 360-degree perspective' resulted in more intense awe experiences than watching normal 2D videos.[16]

Perhaps surprising to some, **social media** can be a great place to encounter more unusual moments of WOW. Some recent awe-inspiring posts I've seen on Twitter include a giant xylophone[17] in the woods of Japan that plays Bach and a video of the surface of Venus.[18] There is even a TikTok sensation called 'Try not to WOW' where you can put your WOW to the test by watching incredible and often strange videos from around the world and do your best not to say 'WOW'.

WOW 101: Learn about what is around you, right now. The process of wrapping your mind around a new concept is called cognitive accommodation, a key component of awe. So, if you take the time to grapple with a new, big idea for you – say quantum physics, you are likely to have a moment of WOW.

'How can a three-pound mass of jelly that you can hold in your palm imagine angels, contemplate the meaning of infinity, and even question its own place in the cosmos? Especially awe-inspiring is the fact that any single brain, including yours, is made up of atoms that were forged in the hearts of countless, far-flung stars billions of years ago. These particles drifted for eons and light-years until gravity and change brought them together here, now. These atoms now form a conglomerate, your brain, that can not only ponder the very stars that gave it birth but can also think about its own ability to think and wonder about its own ability to wonder. With the arrival of humans, it has been said, the universe has suddenly become conscious of itself. This, truly, it the greatest mystery of all.'

– VS Ramachandran[19]

One easy way to bring WOW to your everyday, is to **check you know how things** work around you. The clouds forming up above? How does that happen? The butterfly flying by, how did it grow? The waves coming into shore, how does the tide work? This is a way to transform simple curiosity, into discovery and WOW. And who knows where it might lead? René Descartes and Isaac Newton had fascinations with rainbows which led them to figure out the physics of light.[20]

Even the most of boring of everyday products can produce awe when presented in a unique way. In one study, people experienced awe when they watched a slow-motion video of drops of coloured water falling into a bowl of milk.[21]

Consider that with the mere flick of a switch you can illuminate a room with light or have the television show of your choice beamed into your home.

Read facts and figures. For example, our cells 'know' how to develop into a fully-fledged human being from the union of an egg and sperm. In most instances, our lungs breathe, hearts beat and brains process information without any effort on our parts. Our body's natural intelligence helps us to fight off illness and compensate for injuries. Nerve impulses travel to and from the brain at speeds of up to 250 miles per hour. Your body produces 25 million new cells each second. The Earth is spinning at approximately 1,000 mph (but we don't feel it)!

'The feeling of awed wonder that science can give us is one of the highest experiences of which the human psyche is capable. It is a deep aesthetic passion to rank with the finest that music and poetry can deliver. It is truly one of the things that make life worth living and it does so, if anything, more effectively if it convinces us that the time we have for living is quite finite.'

– Richard Dawkins[22]

It might seem impossible but try and **engineer more WOW into your everyday tasks and chores**, taking a few moments extra to creatively cut fruit and vegetables for snacks, or be inspired by Marie Kondo to fold your clothes so they are beautifully presented in your drawers. Or maybe not.

WOW journeys, your commute and regular walks and trips. When you are travelling, think about how you can bring more WOW into your day. It might be difficult to imagine this when you are on the 0613 to London Paddington, but I promise you it is possible.

Whether it is the route you take, the type of transport you choose, or the mindset you adopt, journeys; both well-travelled and new are ripe for WOW experiences. From the commute to the school run, to the trip to the supermarket to the walk with the dog, through to more leisurely travels and holiday trips. WOWs on the road are there for the taking. In their landmark study of awe published in 2003, Keltner and Haidt described how to get more awe out of an everyday hike by taking time to deepen your thinking about the experience.[23] **Start to look for patterns in nature**, take a moment to think about what's vast. You might consider making a habit of **going for 'awe walks'**. In a recent study,[24] Keltner and his colleagues found that older adults assigned to take weekly 15-minute awe walks reported greater increases in positive emotions and decreases in distress in their day-to-day lives than did those assigned to a control walk condition. Easy ways to getting the most out of an awe walk, include breathing deeply, and shifting your awareness to what's around you.[25]

Another way to find WOW in your everyday is to **change your perspective on a place**; the two key ingredients we are looking for here are 1) a sense of vastness 2) changing your perspective or seeing things differently. For example, climb a hill and look at your hometown, get to a higher vantage point than normal. So, whether that is walking up a steep hill or hiking up a mountain or climbing to the top of a church tower or even skyscraper or multi-storey carpark, take a moment get up there and take in the view. Note: This could even be from a webcam!

We know one key hunting ground, or opportunity for WOW is through **learning and discovery**. So why not recreate the components of our childhood years; opportunities to learn, experiment, be creative, play, discover, problem solve and be inspired, entertained and in awe.

It might be as simple as watching one TED talk per day or listening to music of a different genre than what you are used to as you cook, to visit a museum, exhibition or gallery in your lunchbreak or watch a film, play or performance you know nothing about.

One idea might be to have your own 'school' subject of the week and challenge yourself or even your wider family to share WOWs they have discovered on that subject, whether it is physics, geography, history or literature.

We even set up a friends WhatsApp group (yes, another one) where we shared our WOWs, it was like a book club, but instead we shared facts which had WOW-ed us. (I love the idea of the WOW Club.)

Take time to remember what you loved to do as a child. What were your hobbies, passions and interests? As we know, as children we are a pure version of our 'self', so why not try and revisit some of these activities and pursuits?

I've found that parenting is a great source of fact-finding WOWs, both because I experience awe second-hand when my son understands something new for the first time, but also because human development (how he grows taller, learns and develops each day) is awe-inspiring, full stop! Children are masters of WOW, it comes so easily to them, but they are also subjects of WOW, watching how they learn, grow and change in front of our eyes is awe-inspiring. Remembering children as babies, and then fast forwarding to when they can talk, think and walk is simply incredible.

The WOW trail. What starts off as one simple WOW can often lead to more WOWs. A childlike curiosity can be appeased these days with a simple Google search, and deep diving for more information can lead to discovering more incredible information which leads to WOW after WOW after WOW. Make time for these follow-up WOWs, if you can, as it is a great way to extend the experience.

Sharing your WOW with others. When we uncover new and 'WOW' information, we can save it to share at the next given opportunity (and we all know that sharing is caring). Share your WOW with others and let them experience that moment through you.

Don't forget you can **relive your WOW memories**. For a 'WOW on-demand' you can check out the WOW folder of photographs on your phone to engineer a moment of WOW, right now. Through practices such as mindfulness or just sitting quietly and closing your eyes, you might be able to think about past moments of WOW and allow the feelings from the original experience, to wash over you.

You could consider **starting a WOW journal** where you reflect on moments of WOW, or you could take some time to think of holidays, experiences and moments which made you say WOW. Where were you? Who was there? How did you feel? Why not write about them? When you start documenting and thinking about WOW, you might begin to notice all the places it shows up in your everyday life. You might naturally experience awe more often as you start to pay attention to it, similar to how people often feel more gratitude once they begin a gratitude journal.

'Dashed hopes and good intentions. Good, better, best, bested.'

– Edward Albee – Who's Afraid of Virginia Woolf

Chapter 14.

Find your own WOW

It might seem strange that it has taken until almost the end of the book to get to a chapter called 'Find your own WOW', but there is a reason for that. So far, I have explained how Find Your WOW was born, what I learnt from teaching mindfulness to over 15,000 children and how it helped me unlock what adults lose as they get older, and children have naturally in abundance. I explored why I believe it is easier for children to grasp the ancient life skill of meditation than adults. Then I explored why this might be, when and how we lose our childlike awe and wonder, and the link between the two.

We have looked at the WOW framework and how it can help you to uncover moments of WOW in your day, and why it is important for our health and happiness that we have awe and wonder and WOW at all.

Now we are talking about **YOU**.

In the last chapter I gave you some simple ideas, techniques and exercises to engineer moments of WOW into your day, and how, if you add up all of those fleeting moments, you will be doing enough to feel the benefits to your health and happiness.

But ideas are one thing, doing it is another. **You will need to have a permissive mindset** to make the time, to practise, to allow the experiences, to be prepared to limit the distractions, to quieten the ego and Find Your WOW. Later in this chapter, I will give you some advice on how you can 'landgrab' and make time for WOW in your every day.

With the little wows sorted, what about the big ones? What about the WOWs that only you will appreciate? Those once in a decade or even once in a lifetime WOWs. What if you want to make some bigger changes to your life? How can Find Your WOW help you now?

In his research into happiness, Jonathan Ruch describes a 'happiness graph' which is shaped a little like a smile.[1] It starts at the top, with our happiest point in childhood, slowly descends in a curve until midlife of around 40–50 years old, until it begins to start creeping back up at retirement until our very oldest age.[2] Comedian Dylan Moran puts life down to four stages 'Child, failure, old and dead.'[3]

But perhaps we start our life with high hopes and dreams, and we gradually realise those are unlikely to be fulfilled.

Middle age, or midlife might be the low point of happiness, but it often brings with it a new sense of realism, an appreciation and gratitude for the present moment, a determination to enjoy life, and thus begin a search for more happiness, and WOW.

That brings us to the subjective side to Find Your WOW. These WOWs are just for you. If I was to show 50 people the same undulating mountain vista, the likelihood is that most of them would stand there open-mouthed in awe and wonder and say WOW. Job done.

But what about those moments, personal to you, which will conjure up those feelings of awe and wonder and make you, and maybe only you, say WOW. The moments in which I might say WOW, might leave you nonplussed, and vice versa. Many of your WOWs are likely to be based on your own personal circumstances, experiences, interests, values and life story and could well be linked to your purpose.

**Life is made up of highs and lows;
little WOWs and big WOWs.**

Throughout your life you will experience many moments of little WOWs. These WOWs are not necessarily life changing, and maybe not even particularly memorable, but they are an essential part of day-to-day living, and the ongoing maintenance of the enjoyment of life, little moments of joy that make up the fabric of your happiness, health and well-being.

These WOWs are likely to be made up of your hobbies, passions and personal pursuits and rituals. Some of these might be inspired by your childhood or drawn from memories and experiences in your life story. These little WOWs should be readily available, and regular in occurrence. They are the backbone when it comes to Find Your WOW.

Bigger WOWs lie elsewhere. These are the most grand of all the WOWs, they could be life affirming, life changing or life enhancing in some way. These are likely to be the WOWs you thought about when I asked you to think of an example of the last time you said WOW. Most of these WOWs are likely to be in some way engineered or at least semi-engineered. These WOWs are about hitting goals you have set for yourself, following your dreams, achieving ambitions and aligned with your purpose.

You can use the WOW framework to both increase a sense of awareness which will enable you to explore all these areas for potential WOW experiences in your life, be they big or small.

Many people I spoke to when researching for the book who are in the midlife bracket (forties to fifties, and I fall into that category by the way) have described feeling a sense of losing their way, their identity and some even questioning their purpose, often coming at a time when their children are looking at leaving home and going to college, university, travelling or moving into their own place. Some had lost businesses, and a few had gone bankrupt, others had found they had been made redundant or had fallen out of love with a career they had been in for ten or more years.

Some had relationship issues and were considering divorce; others had found themselves suddenly caring for older relatives. Some had recently lost a parent; others were dealing with the symptoms of the menopause at the same time as navigating the teenage years with their children. A few had become sick or ill and were dealing with the treatment or healing process, whilst also trying to keep things normal for the family. All of them, all of us, had lived through the effects of a global pandemic.

What's certain is that we all, whatever our age, whoever we are, whatever our background and wherever we live in the world, will have a time in our life when we start to have existential thoughts, perhaps to question why we are here and what are we doing, we will examine our priorities, our balance and maybe our role and purpose in life. Or if we are not asking ourselves this, we might at least know someone who is going through this process.

When researching for this book, I discovered a beautiful Japanese concept that was new to me, called ikigai. I will just give you a brief introduction here, as it is a useful point of reference when exploring the idea of one's purpose and meaning within life. Ikigai (ee-key-guy) combines the terms iki, meaning 'alive' or 'life' and gai, meaning 'benefit' or 'worth' in other words, that which gives your life worth, meaning or purpose. Ikigai is similar to the French term 'raison d'être' or 'reason for being.'

One of the leading authorities on the subject of ikigai is Ken Mogi, a neuroscientist and author based in Tokyo.[4] For Ken, there are five pillars of ikigai one can work through to try and gain some awareness, reflection and clarity on our purpose which is linked to what we are good at, what is important to us, our priorities and what we might be able to offer the world.

1. **Starting small:** Taking the first steps, simplifying and looking for small ways to find purpose and joy. These

initial steps are part of a process or journey towards a bigger goal

2. **Releasing yourself:** Negating the burden of the self and accessing the state of flow

3. **Harmony and sustainability:** Having modesty, respect for society, understated beauty and affection for nature

4. **The joy of little things:** Enjoying the simple moments of happiness and pleasure in your everyday

5. **Being in the here and now:** Being mindful and knowing that the present moment is all you have

Ken writes about the personal rituals that we all have in our life, and within our communities, which are unique to us, bring us joy and are aligned to our purpose. He describes the sushi chefs, fruit farmers and fishermen taking enormous pride in doing small things to a very high standard, because it brings them joy and meaning in the world. As you can see, there are some obvious similarities between ikigai and the WOW framework.

Throughout this book we have talked a lot about negating the sense of self, or releasing your EGO, it is also fundamental in accessing the state of FLOW. The final pillar of ikigai is being in the present, which is the same as the mindfulness element of NOW. The other aspects of ikigai are all hunting grounds for WOW experiences including taking pleasure and joy from simple, small things, looking for beauty (even in the mundane) being curious about life and having an affection for nature.

Interestingly, Ken draws a comparison between finding purpose in adulthood and starting by doing small things which is the hallmark of childhood, he says: 'When you are young, you cannot start things in a big way. Whatever you do, it does not matter much to the world. You need to start small. What you have in abundance is open-mindedness and curiosity. Children are inquisitive, determined and passionate.' 'Youthfulness of mind is important in ikigai, but so is commitment and passion, however seemingly insignificant your goal is.'

Find your own WOW is subjective and personal, and that's the point. You might find and cultivate your own WOW, grow it secretly and slowly, until one day it bears a quite original fruit.

In Japan there are so many wonderful concepts that can be linked to WOW including wabi-sabi, a world view centred on the acceptance of transience and imperfection, the impermanent and incomplete. As we explored earlier, the Japanese hold a belief of the ephemeral; something that does not last, the transient, the imperfect and impermanent. Much like the admiration of the annual spring cherry blossom (Hanami) and one of my favourites is a concept of kodawari which means having personal pride in what you do, however small or seemingly insignificant it might with an excessive level of detail for something for which you have a passion for. It might be that this concept can also inspire us when it comes to finding your own WOW.

There are some good examples of kodawari in my

hometown of Bath. A couple of my favourite coffee shops happen to combine selling coffee with the other passions or interests of their proprietors. Right in the heart of the city centre, there is Chapter 22 Roots & Records which has a little coffee bar as a part of a wonderful shop which sells plants and vinyl records. They also sometimes have live music events. Secondly, there's Bijou Bikeworks, which is situated on the cycle path into town, down by the river, close to where I live. The owner not only has an incredible passion for selling the very best coffee which you can enjoy sitting on a little terrace outside of his shop, he also has a joint interest in fixing bicycles which he does from the shop next door, which is very handy when you are on one of the busiest cycle routes in the area. One of my favourite 'WOW-Inducing' shops is a plant-lovers' heaven called Botanica Studio with floor-to-ceiling greenery and it smells just divine. I was lucky enough to work for some time at Aardman Animations in Bristol where I looked after publicity for the stop-motion character, Morph. To see the animators in action was just breath-taking and I was completely in awe of their talents. A special mention goes to the Matchbox Barbershop & Salon, 'probably the smallest salon in England' which has simply one barber's chair in a tiny shop space in a corner of Bath, I just love it.

You can probably think of similar places, where someone has taken their passion and turned it into their life's work. I am always so impressed and inspired when people make this happen and turn it into an effective business, it really is a moment of WOW. Hats off.

Whether it's having the smallest and best sushi restaurant, running an incredible coffee shop, or simply fulfilling your job within an office to do any printing and photocopying to the best of your ability, under kodawari you fulfil that role (however small it is) with huge attention to detail, exceeding all expectations and completing it to a very high standard. To give moments of WOW to yourself and others, have the WOW factor in what you do.

Ken describes some of these kind of businesses in Japan, 'good enough is simply not good enough for them. You could even call it creative insanity, really. They are in search of perfection, on a constant journey of self-improvement.'

In the next section, we are going to use some open-ended questions which might help you in your search to find your own WOW; whether that is a new hobby or interest, or something more substantial such as a career change or redirection. It might be as simple as helping you to identify areas of your life which are out of balance and from this, it will be up to you to make further investigations and research as to how you move forward. I hope it might spark a moment of awareness, inspiration or clarity where you can discover for yourself, something that was there all along.

I encourage you to write down the first answer that comes to mind, all too often we try and give the 'right' answer which is not always aligned with our true self. So, without further ado, grab a pen and let's get started in finding your own WOW. How exciting!

In a moment, you will read 15 questions and I would like

you to try and come up with 15 different times from your life, which best match the question. These should be examples which immediately come to mind, rather than ruminating for too long over each response. Try to give a different example for each, which might be something that has happened in your past, childhood, or from your present-day life.

THE QUESTIONS:

NOW
In this section we are looking for times when you have felt in the moment, and fully present, this might include having a sense of gratitude or connection to others, or a time when you felt happiness.
What made/makes you smile when you are doing it, and feel joy when you think of it? [HAPPINESS]

_____

_____

When did/do you feel most grateful? [SELF FULFILLING/ REWARD]

_____

_____

When did/do you feel the most connected to others? [RELATIONSHIPS]

_____

_____

FOCUS

In this section we are looking for when you find it easy to focus your attention, you are not distracted, and where your skills and talents come naturally, you are self-motivated to start a task, even when you do not have to do it.

What skills or talents came/come easily or naturally to you? [TALENT]

_____

_____

What did/do you excel at even when you were/are not trying? [ABILITIES]

_____

_____

When were/are you least distracted? And could/can easily keep focussed? [FOCUS]

_____

_____

FLOW

In this section we are looking for times when you may have been in the zone or in the flow state. It might be a time when you have felt like you were at one with the activity you were doing, lost track of time and you were completely immersed.

What were/are you doing when you last lost track of time? [FLOW]

_____

_____

What did/do you never get bored with, or enjoy doing without being asked? [ENGAGEMENT/SELF MOTIVATION]

_____

_____

When did/do you feel most creative? [CREATIVITY]

_____

_____

EGO

This is about looking at who you really are, your true self, your personality traits your passions and interests which have perhaps been with you since childhood. We are also looking for what motivates you and what your special gift to the world might be.

What could/can you offer to the world, that means the most to others? [COMMUNITY/SENSE OF ROLE]

_____

_____

What did you enjoy most of all during your childhood? [SELF]

_____

_____

When did/do you feel most alive? [8-YEAR-OLD]

_____

_____

WOW

In this section we are looking for what brings you joy, energises you and gives you a sense of achievement.

When did/do you feel most energised? [CHARGING ENERGY]

_____

_____

When were you most proud of something you've done? [GOALS AND AMBITIONS]

_____

_____

When did/do you feel most fulfilled? [PURPOSE/REWARD]

_____

_____

Once you have your answers, you can move to identifying the key themes which are popping up for you. What is important for this section is that you are as generic as possible as you are trying to look for overarching principles which might guide you in your search to find your own WOW; whether that is big or small.

IDENTIFY YOUR KEY THEMES AROUND:
- The emotions that you feel
- Locations where situations have occurred
- Common experiences you raise
- Relationships and connections to others
- Skills and abilities you have (non-specific)
- Motivations
- Priorities
- Where you feel most fulfilled and a sense of achievement

Whatever you decide to do with your responses to these questions, and to this book in general, it might just encourage you to rekindle a passion from childhood, realise that you want to spend more time outdoors, or even retrain for a new career.

We can all have moments where we feel a little bit lost, stale or jaded in the status quo and as if every day is the same. One of the greatest gifts Find Your WOW can give you is the awareness of how you are feeling, and that you have the ability to start making a change. Starting small might be important, taking the baby WOWs towards making a bigger one. Persistence, consistency, practice and effort might be required along the way, but it will be worth it.

Remember, moments of WOW do not have to change the

world, they just need to change your world. And they might not last more than a fleeting moment, but they will be just enough to relight that fire within, to remind you of who you are, and what is important in life. That might be as simple as cooking a dish from childhood which when you taste it, takes you all the way back to that time. It might be something bigger. Only you can decide.

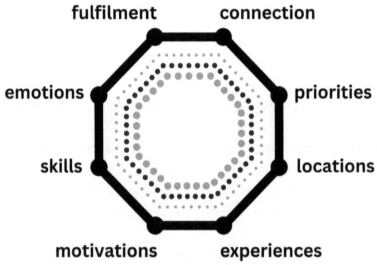

© Lucy Stone

TEN WAYS TO MAKE TIME FOR WOW

1. Diarise a weekly big dose of WOW. Try to make time each week for a planned WOW; this might be organising to go for a walk in nature, booking a ticket to watch a live performance or being with people you find inspirational. This might be as little as 30 minutes or a few hours. It is important that you know you will

be (pretty much) guaranteed a good dose of WOW each week, which you can reflect on.

2. Make time for micro dosing WOWs in your everyday. As we know, life is more commonly made up of small moments of joy and WOW which are often unplanned, and spontaneous. We might even need to force them to arise, by lingering for a little longer on say, a beautiful flower, view or the taste of a meal or drink.

3. Accept imperfections, there will not be WOWs each time you set out to engineer or plan one.

4. Prioritise pleasure. It is all too easy to do chores over taking time to experience WOW and of course you will do both but look for ways to bring WOW into your more mundane tasks, and make sure you make time for pleasure too.

5. Understand the importance of what you are doing, like anything which is good for us, we know it is good for us (eating well, exercising etc.) but we can't always, and don't always make time for them. Understanding why WOW moments are important for our health and well-being (and that of those around us) might be all the motivation we need to make time for them.

6. Understand how precious time is. Time is the one thing we will all eventually run out of and that, we cannot control. How we decide to spend our time; our boundaries, our priorities and our experiences have a huge effect on the quality of our life, our emotional, mental and physical health and so much more.

7. Change your routine, we can get caught in a rut sometimes. In a never-ending regime of admin, chores and schedules, we can mix things up a little. We might not be able to change WHAT we have to do, but we might be able to change HOW we do it. The commute, the school run, the route to places we visit each week, the meals we eat, our exercise routine and where we shop.

8. Lower your screen time. FULL STOP.

9. Un-diarise, make time for spontaneity, try and leave free space in your week to say yes to invitations, act on your needs and try things.

10. Piggyback, explore how you might be able to experience WOW on the way to, or on the way from appointments, or whilst you are doing all the things you have to do in your week. Have to go to a meeting or an appointment in a new area of town? Why not look up the history or visit a gallery or park whilst you are there? Have to drive somewhere to pick up something you have bought on an online marketplace? Why not take in some nature, or visit a friend who lives nearby? You get the idea.

'The world is full of magic things, patiently waiting for our senses to grow sharper.'

– William Butler Yeats

Chapter 15.

The new WOW order –
The world where we all find
more WOW

So, what happens now? You understand the framework of what makes up a WOW experience, you might comprehend why WOW might be important for you, and perhaps you are beginning to see where you might be able to fit opportunities for WOW within your life.

In this chapter, we will look at how finding WOW might become an integral part of a new world, in what I have called The new WOW order. Rather than looking at specific ways to find WOW, I will explore the overarching principles in the Find Your WOW mindset to create opportunities for WOW experiences.

Of course, it is not practical to walk around in a daze, saying WOOWWWW at everything you see, we would probably be arrested. We all need to go about our normal life without our friends and family disowning us, getting fired or not getting anything done. But, that said, many of us are living with a limited amount of WOW in our everyday, and there are some very simple habits and ideas to engineer just a little more WOW into your life. And that's got to be a good thing, right?

As we have already discovered, WOW experiences come from three main sources:

- **Spontaneous WOWs** – For example you turn a corner and there is a breath-taking view which stops you in your tracks. These to a certain extent are uncontrolled, the rarest but perhaps the most memorable and intense WOW experiences. Not only are they WOW-inducing, but they would also have the biggest element of surprise or shock, you are likely to gasp or take a sharp intake of breath.

- **Planned WOWs** – For example you want to experience a WOW moment, so you intentionally apply the framework to something. You might simply stare at a vase of flowers or a candle so you force yourself to be curious in the hope a WOW will follow. These WOWs are often planned, known about in advance and intentional. They might be less impactful or emotional, but are perhaps the most important to consider as during these experiences you are practising your response, openness and propensity for when the other two, stronger WOWs arise.

- **Situational WOWs** – This is where you put yourself in a situation which might create a WOW such going to a concert, taking a walk in the forest, and then suddenly bang! It happens. You can engineer an opportunity for WOW, with the hope that a WOW experience will follow, but it also might not. You can book the ticket to a performance and try to immerse yourself in the experience, then just sit tight and wait for the WOW to happen. If it arrives, you can apply the framework to ensure that you are maximising the impact of the WOW on your mind, well-being and memory bank.

So far, we have focussed on the framework as a tool to immerse yourself in experiences, to encounter more WOW in your life. In the coming chapters we will explore how you might adopt the framework as a way of life and as a mindset. We will also look at ways to plan (and semi-plan) more WOW in our everyday.

When I was teaching children in schools, it was often the most surprising and seemingly normal experiences that would conjure up a WOW. That's because for a child they are often experiencing or witnessing this 'thing' for the very first time. As we grow older, we might feel as if we have **'seen' everything before**, but of course we haven't. Whether we are witnessing something we have experienced a hundred times before, or encountering something new, we can try and look through the eyes of a child, to see the world differently.

When we think of a moment of WOW as a 'mini break for the mind', we don't need to visit far-flung exotic places for a holiday. Unlike holidays which are taken rarely, **these moments should be frequent**, as many in a day as possible, even if these moments of WOW last only a few seconds. You will be amazed at the cumulative effects on your mind. We are not looking for life-changing experiences, but all added together, they might just change your life.

Here are my 'quick WOW wins' that you can weave into your day.

1. New experiences
2. 'Old' experiences, done differently
3. Being in nature
4. Being with people you are in awe of
5. Experiences where you can use as many of your senses as possible

DONE REGULARLY. YOU NEED TO PRACTISE. PRACTISE. PRACTISE. PRACTISE.

Before we start looking at specific ideas of how to weave WOW into your every day, let's recap on the framework:

1. **NOW.** Be present, slow down your pace, you won't Find Your WOW if you're in a rush. Take a slower approach to even the most mundane of tasks; as you water your plants, tenderly check for new growth or weeds. When you are eating, take time to ponder how that food has reached you. If you make this slower, more mindful approach, your norm, you are creating the best climate for WOWs to emerge. Take some deep breaths and allow the experience to unfold.

2. **FOCUS.** Disconnect from technology and pour your attention on to what you are doing. Turn off notifications, step away from the screen, remove yourself from other people if necessary. Try to limit distractions, whether

that is internal or external, and take time to enjoy the moment, using as many of your senses as possible.

3. **FLOW.** When you catch yourself feeling a WOW moment, try and go with it, and let it sit with you for as long as possible. The two main WOW killers are distraction or loss of FOCUS, and EGO where you start to question, analyse or judge the experience. Fight these urges to kill your WOW. Linger in wonder for as long as you can.

4. **EGO.** If you start to hear your conscience, inner voice or critic chirping, then try to bat it away by calmly remaining focussed. One way to do this is to dial up your senses a little more; tuning into the detail, colour and texture of where you are. What can you hear, see, smell? Allow yourself to sink into your senses which connect us with the outside world and discover a little more awe and wonder and turn the WOW volume up to 11. Forget about yourself and the social barriers, the judgement around you. E.g. it's easier to dance and let go when you have a couple of drinks and your social barriers fall.

5. **WOW.** When you feel the WOW arrive, be open to being inspired; what comes into your mind? What do you notice? Do you have goosebumps? How do you feel?

Important: Don't worry if some days you just don't feel it, there will be other times for WOW.

There is one key area for WOW, which I have already touched upon but would like to dedicate some more time to and that is when we experience moments of WOW with other people, maybe within a large crowd. You might consider that WOW should be a personal or somehow individual experience, and of course it will be. But the effects of a WOW can be magnified and intensified, if you are with the RIGHT people. We talked in the previous chapter about WOW killers, how some people around you might have a negative effect on a WOW experience, draining the joy and fulfilment from the moment. But find the right people, and it can have the opposite effect.

Have you ever been at a music concert or festival or sporting event or listened to someone give a talk or speech, and you've been so immersed in the moment that you don't notice anything of what's happening around you? When the crowd starts singing or cheering, you sing and cheer along with them, you feel strangely emotional, you have goosebumps, you are completely in awe of what you are watching. Maybe you felt inspired, overcome with admiration for what you are witnessing but you are also alongside others who are all feeling the same way. I feel sure if you have ever been in this situation, you may have said WOW, during or after this moment. Then this was likely to be a moment of WOW.

Let's look at what happened here, let's say it's a musical performance; if you booked the tickets, it was a planned WOW, if you were out for a walk and heard music and intentionally went towards it, it was situational WOW, if you stumbled across the event purely by chance it was an unintentional, or spontaneous WOW.

The next step was you had a **permissive mindset**, you made some decisions to take time and adopt the WOW framework. You stopped and paused in the moment, the music captured your attention, and you began to focus all of your attention on the performance. Maybe you stopped talking to your friend, your phone is in your pocket, you begin to immerse yourself in the performance. You start to forget everything else; you don't notice the weather, you momentarily feel your phone vibrate in your pocket with a message but ignore it and focus back immediately on what is happening in front of you. If you have a fleeting thought that perhaps I should look at my phone in case it is something important or have a pang of guilt for being there and not doing something else, you notice the thought but simply bat it away. You are fully immersed now, singing and moving along with the crowd around you. You have a sense that you are a part of something bigger, a community and your worries momentarily disappear. Finally, at the end of the performance you say, 'WOW that was amazing'. You might get out your phone and take a photograph of the performer and the stage to capture the memory, or take a selfie with friends so that on those less WOW days, you can relive this moment, and this feeling of WOW.

The WOW happened because of the focus and attention you poured into whatever you were watching, you were flowing to the point where you might have felt as if you were a part of the event itself. Nothing else mattered, you didn't think about anything else, you did not critique yourself or the performance, you were just absorbed. Soaked in WOW. But the feeling was likely magnified because people around you were also having the same feeling and experience. It has been found that your flow state can be triggered or magnified when you are with others, in a crowd or audience.

Whether you are on a protest march with a few hundred thousand other people through the streets of your capital city, all marching for the same cause, or in a crowd celebrating a World Series, or at a festival where you danced late into the night, the contagious euphoria you felt has a name: 'collective effervescence'. Despite it being incredibly relevant today, the term was in fact coined over a hundred years ago by a French sociologist, Émile Durkheim. It refers to that glowy, giddy feeling where your sense of self slackens, yielding to a connection with your fellow, synchronised humans.

More recently, other studies have been carried out on the concept and psychologist Shira Gabriel's research,[1] has looked at how these effervescent experiences fill the human need for belonging. In a time when the number of us who are part of a religious community is on the decline,[2] often these mass events are the only times we can become part of something on a bigger scale with other humans. Gabriel's research looked at how customs as ancient as pilgrimages and feast days, and modern as protests and sports, help people to lead happier, connected and more personally meaningful lives.

The next time you are considering your opportunities for WOW, explore how you might experience these with other people, either in a **collective sense** such as being part of a crowd at a festival, or whether you choose your WOW warriors, those people who share the same outlook, mindset and attitude as you, to experience something together in a group which may well magnify the experience for you all. Just leave the WOW killers and drainers at home.

Curiosity plays a huge part in the WOW framework, even the most mundane experience might become a WOW if you just apply a little more awe, wonder and curiosity to what you are facing. I started this book by talking about how the children I have taught over the past six years or so have been the inspiration for Find Your WOW, how they are naturally curious about everything around them, and how as adults we have lost this. As we have explored, children have open-mindedness, big dreams and curiosity in abundance.

In the last chapter, we explored the crossover between ikigai, what brings you joy and gets you out of bed every morning, and WOW. In his Little Book of Ikigai, Japanese author Ken Mogi describes how in post-war Japan, the Supreme Commander of the Allied Powers, General Douglas MacArthur famously referred to Japan as a 'nation of 12-year-olds'. He was referring to the immature nature of Japan's democracy at the time, and it was said as a derogatory statement. But if you take that a youthful mindset filled with curiosity is a plus in life, then this could be taken as a compliment. Perhaps, ikigai with its youthfulness of mind, commitment and passion to a goal (however insignificant) like WOW, makes a Peter Pan of all of us, which might be a good thing.

As adults we are often rushing around and don't make or take time to be mindful. Part of the new WOW order is about adjusting your pace in life to **allow time for WOW**. I don't just mean setting aside some time each week or even day to experience moments of WOW, although I do think this is a good thing, I mean an overall slowing down in life to try and appreciate what is around you. As Viktor Frankl,[3] Austrian psychiatrist and psychotherapist, stressed, 'All you ever have is the present moment'.

Back in Japanese culture, they have a philosophy of ichigo ichie ('for this time only' which literally means one time, one encounter). It originally comes from the tea ceremony tradition and the respect of the **ephemeral** character of any encounters with people, things or events in life. Understanding the ephemeral nature of life is a huge lightbulb moment when it comes to WOW. Once we appreciate that this moment will never ever be repeated, it can unlock a whole new way of thinking about experiences. I know it might be difficult to conceive this when you are on the 0613 train to London Paddington for the third day in a row, travelling to sit at a desk, in the same office, alongside the same people as every other day for the past who-knows-how-many years. But it's true, this moment has never happened before, not in the same way, not with the same circumstances, not with the same context or feeling and it's our job to notice how it is different. Practising mindfulness can play its part in helping us to increase our awareness of our present moment, to tune into our surroundings and to notice and to be grateful for the small things.

Ken Mogi says: 'Because an encounter is ephemeral, it must be taken seriously. Life, after all, is filled with things that only happen once. The realisation of the "oneness" of life's encounters and pleasures provides the foundations for the Japanese concept of ikigai, and the Japanese philosophy of life.' When you take notice of the small details of life, nothing is the same, nothing is repeated, this moment will never happen again. When you start to adopt this mindset, even the simplest moments become WOW.

Whatever you do, might not make a huge impact to the world. One of my favourite sayings which I preach to my son is 'You might not change the world, but you can change your world or the world around you'. But that is not always the case, take Greta Thunberg, who started a weekly Friday protest outside of the Swedish parliament, which led to a movement with children all over the world doing the same thing to raise awareness of environmental issues and their feeling of frustration and insignificance. If we consider the power of 'collective effervescence', the school strike protest took a small act of one 15-year-old girl and slowly began to take a disproportionate effect. Beyond even the wildest dreams of Greta herself, I am sure.

TEN PRINCIPLES TO ADOPT FOR A NEW WOW ORDER:

1. **You have not seen everything before.** Even if you think you have, see what you are doing with new eyes, in a new way, with an almost childlike approach.

2. **Look for moments of WOW regularly.** However they come; uncontrolled, engineered or semi-engineered, try and experience a moment of WOW daily if possible.

3. **Practise applying the WOW framework in your everyday life,** apply it to the most mundane of tasks e.g. housework, or chores, in your job or commute or simply staring at a view. By practising and looking for hidden WOWs in the everyday, you will more easily slip in a WOW moment when a more extravagant experience arises.

4. Look for opportunities to have **collective or group** WOW experiences as this can magnify the intensity of the feeling.

5. Have a **permissive mindset** to WOW, make the time, book the tickets, meet up with others, say yes – within your boundaries and allow yourself to experience.

6. Adopt a **mindset of curiosity;** ask questions, research, discover, experiment, don't always plan, do things differently, play, be creative, make mistakes, fail, learn, enjoy!

7. **Make time for WOW,** diarise time for WOW, undiarise your life to create space and time for opportunities, experiences and spontaneity.

8. Remember the **ephemeral nature of life,** this moment is unique and will never be repeated.
9. Having an **awareness** of where and how to Find Your WOW, what gives joy and what you are passionate about, and of course how you are feeling.
10. **Change your world, not the world** but do not underestimate the impact of small actions and the ripple effect of your new WOW order on others. (See coming chapter on Can WOW really save your mind?)

A reminder, your five quick wow wins are:
1. New experiences
2. 'Old' experiences with new eyes; mindfulness and childlike curiosity
3. Being in nature
4. Being with people you are in awe of
5. Experiences where you can use as many of your senses as possible

'Every day set a few moments aside to think and feel how amazing it is to be alive.'

– Marty Rubin

Chapter 16.

Can WOW really save your mind?

We have looked at how the individual pillars of WOW; being in the NOW, keeping our FOCUS, finding FLOW and letting go of our EGO are all beneficial, for our health and well-being. WOW is a concept I have developed, so we have also explored how the recent research in the science of awe and wonder might be a useful comparison.

Before I go any further, I would like to say one thing. Maybe you are reading this and going through a difficult time. Or perhaps you are thinking this is not for me, and maybe that's true right now.

There are benefits to be taken from just following the first two pillars of WOW, the mindfulness and the flow state. Whole books have been written about these two subjects alone, and there's some great ones recommended in my reference list. It's also useful to be aware of the main killers of WOW; (and indeed killers of mindfulness and the flow state) namely, a loss of FOCUS, and EGO. There are also masses of books written about those two subjects (again, some of my favourites are listed in my reference list).

But for me, there is an interconnection between all these subjects, which have led me to this point, and more specifically to write this book now. None of these subjects as a standalone are particularly new, but based on my unique teaching experience and research, I have brought them all together and developed the concept of WOW.

Moments of WOW are likely to have a broad range of benefits for you as the individual who is experiencing them, but as we will learn there is a likely ripple effect that will occur, which might well impact other people. When we experience WOW, because of its link to mindfulness and the flow state, we are likely to feel a sense of happiness. We are so immersed in the moment that all other thoughts and worries have momentarily disappeared, our stress levels are lowered, and we feel a greater connection to others and the world.

Interestingly, other health benefits might arise from the 'surprise' nature of WOWs particularly those which are uncontrolled or unexpected, including a renewed sense of connection or positive outlook, improvement to memory and recall and how we learn. Finally in this chapter, we will delve deeper into how when one person experiences a moment of WOW, that feeling can be transferred to other people, in some magical 'WOW exchange'.

Built on my observations and research, WOW encapsulates what so many of us adults have lost with age, experience and lifestyle. If only we could recapture some of the childlike awe and wonder and curiosity of life, we once had. It might help us to develop a deeper connection to experiences and people, to keep our attention in the here and now, (without worrying about the past or the future) and let go of who we think we should be. We might feel better in our mind and even a little more human.

The world we are living in right now has been through, and continues to go through, incredible societal change. The acceleration of change is illustrated by the rise of Artificial Intelligence, global shifts in power and a mental health 'epidemic' across the whole spectrum of age groups. We spend so much of our life on screens and devices, our planet is suffering, robots are replacing humans in many roles, and the jobs that our children will do, might not even exist yet. There is an economic, political and digital revolution which as humans we are constantly adjusting to.

WHAT PART CAN FIND YOUR WOW HAVE IN ALL OF THIS?

Is it pathetic to think that finding a little more awe and wonder in your every day and being a little more curious could make the slightest difference to your life, or the lives of those around you? But surely it must.

We know from the growth in the size of the mindfulness app industry, that more of us are turning to ancient practices such as meditation to help cope with the pressures of the modern world; to slow down our pace of life, to help us get a better night's sleep and to manage our stress levels.

We might think that **being mindful** or even adopting a regular meditation practice is a purely personal endeavour with individual rewards, and that's certainly partly the case due to the physical and mental health benefits that come with practising mindfulness.

Research has shown that those who practise mindfulness regularly are more community spirited, make decisions more consciously, have a greater connection to the natural world and the wider planet and greater empathy towards others, even those we do not know or have not even met.

Being in the here and now and negation of the self, are two of the key elements in the Find Your WOW framework. If we adopt WOW as an overall approach to life, we can behave better towards other people and the planet. Potentially this could have wider consequences. Often when we have a moment of WOW, a feeling of gratitude and connection will follow as an after effect and then we are more likely to act for the greater good.

The **focus and attention** spans of children and adults are at an all-time low. Whilst some daydreaming and mind wandering is healthy and natural and required by the brain in its cycle of recovery, many of us report the complete inability to focus on anything for a reasonable period, with procrastination and distraction always a temptation. Engaging in activities that force us to focus our attention, can train (and retrain) the brain to help keep focussed in even the most boring of tasks.

Why not use the WOW framework as an exercise to train your focus, which might just save your mind from a world of distraction and procrastination. We can find the planned and situational WOW moments, where we can use our self-discipline, intention and creativity to discover the hidden WOWs in our day. Each time we do this, we are growing and developing the areas of the brain we use for focus.

When you experience WOW, you will likely have feelings of **surprise or even shock**. This is felt most strongly in a spontaneous WOW, where you had no expectation of what would happen. But are surprises good for the mind? When an unexpected event happens, there is a release of noradrenaline within the body, which helps focus the brain's attention and secondly enables us to learn from the event.[1] Your amygdala is activated in a surprising situation as it helps you decide whether the surprise is good for you or not, this part of the brain regulates your fight or flight mechanism. So long as the surprise is not hurtful or negative, it leads to positive emotions which may have a long-lasting effect. If the surprise is pleasant, which hopefully most moments of WOW are, then dopamine is released within the body.

Scientists have found that the part of the brain which is activated in an unexpected situation or surprise is the nucleus accumbens. This **is an extremely important area of pleasure in the brain** and probably the reason why the brain loves surprises (at least at first). It doesn't matter if the surprise is good or bad, as this region lights up every time, activating pleasure mechanisms.

Surprises (and WOWs) are good for the mind and good for the soul.

If an important feature of WOW is the element of surprise, then **WOWs might even help us learn better**. Over the past 50 years, scientists have identified the main factors that enables us to not just learn, but not forget, and surprise is one of them. Maybe introducing an element of WOW and surprise to your learning will ensure the knowledge sticks for a little longer. How often have you read an incredible mind-blowing fact or statistic and said 'WOW'? I bet you remember those far more easily than the less WOW-inducing ones. Perhaps as we get older, by engineering more learning opportunities and continuing to have WOW-inducing experiences, we can save our mind from some of the natural age deterioration we all experience with time.

According to researchers, when something is surprising it is more likely to stay in your memory.[2] This is perhaps why science teachers use vivid and exciting experiments to demonstrate scientific theories, rather than relying on teaching from textbooks. This relationship between learning and surprises in the brain is well documented. Moreover, studies have shown that when an experience occurs around the same time as a surprise they remain in a person's **memory for longer**, this is because of the increased focus and attention from the dopamine which is released. For example, if you have a spontaneous WOW it is more likely to remain as a clear memory than perhaps a situational or planned WOW, where you know more about what is happening and have greater control over the experience.

If we release **dopamine when we are surprised**, what happens when we don't get our fix, or stay living in a wow-less world? Symptoms of dopamine deficiency include; problems with anger, low self-esteem, anxiety, forgetfulness, impulsiveness, social withdrawal, reduced emotions and inability to feel pleasure.

Are we happy when we experience WOW? I would expect so. If we are fully immersed in a moment of WOW, we are likely to be to a greater or lesser extent in the flow state. Mihaly Csikszentmihalyi described the flow state as the optimum state of happiness and where we can thrive in peak performance.

The four main happy hormones which promote positive feelings, including happiness and pleasure include;

- **Dopamine:** Known as the 'feel-good' hormone, dopamine is a neurotransmitter that's an important part of your brain's reward system. It's associated with pleasurable sensations, along with learning, memory and more.[3]

- **Serotonin:** This hormone and neurotransmitter helps regulate your mood as well as your sleep, appetite, digestion, learning ability and memory.[4]

- **Oxytocin:** Often called the 'love hormone',[5] oxytocin is essential for childbirth, breastfeeding and strong parent–child bonding. It can also help promote trust, empathy and bonding in relationships. Levels generally increase with physical affection.

- **Endorphins:** These hormones are your body's natural pain reliever, which your body produces in response to stress or discomfort. Levels may also increase when you engage in reward-producing activities such as eating, working out or having sex.[6]

These hormones help promote happiness and pleasure while reducing depression and anxiety. You can give these feel-good hormones a natural boost with some simple activities. Finding moments of WOW which trigger these hormones will help maximise the chance for finding happiness in WOW.

TEN SIMPLE WAYS TO GET HAPPY IN WOW

1. **Get outside.** Spending time in sunlight[7] is a great way to boost your serotonin level. According to research,[8] exposure to ultraviolet (UV) radiation from the sun can increase the production of serotonin. Especially during the darker months, make sure you see some daylight and perhaps even combine this with Vitamin D.

2. **Exercise** has multiple physical health benefits[9] and has a positive impact on emotional well-being. If you've heard of a 'runner's high',[10] you might already know about the link between exercise and endorphin release. But exercise doesn't just work on endorphins. Regular physical activity can also increase your dopamine and serotonin levels, making it a great option to boost your happy hormones.

3. **Be with friends and other people.** A small 2017 study[11] of medical students found evidence to suggest group

exercise offers more significant benefits than solo exercise. Socialising, calling a friend and laughing can help relieve feelings of anxiety[12] or stress and improve a low mood, by boosting dopamine and endorphin levels. But look out for those who drain your energy and WOW.

4. **Be with your loved one(s).** Simply being attracted to someone can lead to the production of oxytocin. But physical affection, including kissing, cuddling[13] or having sex, also contributes to oxytocin production.[14] Just spending time with someone you care about can also help boost oxytocin production. This can help increase closeness and positive relationship feelings, making you feel happy, blissful or even euphoric.

5. **Be with animals.** If you have a dog, giving your furry friend some affection is a great way to boost oxytocin levels for you and your dog. According to research, owners as well as their pets, see an increase in oxytocin when they interact with each other.

6. **Food!** This tip could hit the happy hormone jackpot. The enjoyment you get from eating something delicious can trigger the release of dopamine along with endorphins. Sharing the meal with someone you love, and bonding over meal preparation, can boost oxytocin levels. Certain foods can also have an impact on hormone levels, so note the following when meal planning for a happy hormone boost:
   - **spicy foods** may trigger endorphin release
   - **yogurt, beans, eggs, meats with low-fat content**

    and almonds are just a few foods linked to dopamine release

- **foods high in tryptophan** have been linked to increased serotonin levels, such as eggs, poultry, salmon, banana, milk, cheese and… chocolate!
- **foods containing probiotics**, such as yogurt, kimchi and sauerkraut, can influence the release and balance of hormones

7. **Music!** This can give more than one of your happy hormones a boost. Listening to instrumental music, especially music that gives you chills, can increase dopamine production in your brain.[15] Simply listening to any music you enjoy may put you in a good mood which can increase serotonin production. You may also experience an endorphin release while performing music, especially in a large group. For example, one study found that choir members experienced increased endorphin release during rehearsals.

8. **Meditation.** Many of the benefits of meditation are linked to increased dopamine production which include improved sleep and reduced stress.

9. **Creativity.** Try to bring elements of creativity into your everyday, this doesn't always mean getting out the watercolours and easel, this could be anything from doodling on a notepad, colouring in or writing in a journal, just creativity for creativity's sake.

10. **Be Playful.** And just like creativity, play just for the sake of it, dance in the kitchen, play games and move around without rules, reason or restriction.

Are you ready for something incredibly fascinating? What if, when you are experiencing a moment of WOW, you could pass that feeling on to someone else, whether you know them or not?

What if WOW could not just save your mind, but the minds of those around you? What if by you finding your WOW, others also found theirs?

In 1996, Italian neuroscientists discovered something exciting. When examining a monkey's brain, they discovered its neurons became active when completing a task. They noticed that the same set of neurons also became active when the monkey observed others doing that same action. These 'mirror neurons'[16] have also been found in humans, in various parts of the brain.[17]

Mirror neurons are activated when someone witnesses an act and performs the very same act themselves, even if it is just in their imagination. Your brain responds to the action as though you were the one to carry it out. Mirror neurons discharge during both the first-hand performance and the second-hand observation of that performance.[18] When you interact with someone, you can often understand the individual's feelings and actions, for example we see someone crying on a film or TV series, we might feel empathy and start crying ourselves. Scientists believe this is one of the ways humans learn and communicate. You might feel empathy, you might feel joy, you might feel WOW.

One easy way to experience this, is by having a conversation with someone. When we are telling or listening to a story, the brain activity between us and our conversation partner starts to align. As we become involved with the story, it becomes real in our mind and body. This is all thanks to mirror neurons.

This concept is important for learning and understanding new knowledge and skills, but also in grasping the actions and intentions of others. It is why humans have the capacity for empathy or need to share the feelings, it is also thought to be why we yawn when others yawn or smile when those around us smile, or why we feel a heightened sense of belonging at a large event such as a rock concert.

At the time of writing this, I have just watched The Cure in concert, in Basel, Switzerland. It is quite possibly one of the most incredible musical experiences of my life. I am familiar with only a tiny proportion of their discography, but I found a lot of the music was almost trance-like, and for one song, they projected the drummer on to the back screen, for his solo performance. For what seemed like hours I was completely transfixed by Jason Cooper as he played the drums in a sort of tribal beat, I watched his face, he was entirely focussed and in the state of flow. Not a single mistake, of course, a powerful spellbinding performance. In some strange way I felt like it was me who was drumming, I was so absorbed in the performance. Is it possible that by me watching Jason in the state of flow, I had somehow matched his neurons and was having the feeling of being in the flow state, without the challenge or skill level? What's more, I was standing in a crowd of thousands of people most of whom were also transfixed in the same way. Time seemed to stand still, and I was thinking about nothing else other than watching him drum. Could it possibly be that the feeling was being magnified because I was in a group or crowd environment? Just as I have explained earlier in the book about 'collective effervescence'.

I am pretty sure as Jason finished his solo when he looked out at the crowd, he would have experienced a moment of WOW. In the audience, many of us would have used that word to describe his performance and were certainly in awe of his talent.

As well as collective effervescence and mirror neurons, there is a third way we can experience another person's moment of WOW, vicariously. Vicarious joy[19] is the ability to feel happy about other people's positive experiences.[20] It can be defined by its focus on the other person's positive experience rather than one's own feeling of positivity, which is sometimes defined as warm glow.[21] Rather, vicarious joy requires the ability to cognitively grasp someone else's emotional state, also referred to as mentalising.[22]

Watching sports[23] or live comedy, listening to a speaker give an inspirational talk or interview on a podcast or even reading about someone else's life, can all bring about vicarious emotions. So perhaps watching someone who is having a WOW-inducing experience, can install a feeling of WOW within us.

WOW ON PRESCRIPTION?

It is already common in the UK to use 'social prescription' as treatment for health conditions. This system provides access to activities which are good for our mental health and well-being including the creative arts, green spaces and experience of caring for animals as an alternative to more traditional medical interventions.

At the time of writing this chapter, the Wildlife Trust has written to the Government to encourage them to commit further support towards the 'Green Prescribing for Mental Health programme'. The Trust emphasises how green prescribing is 'an evidence-based pillar of social prescribing that harnesses the proven health and well-being benefits of spending time in nature' and highlights how the programme generated almost £7 worth of social value for every £1 invested.[24]

Perhaps, if we can self-medicate with moments of WOW, we can also feel a little happier, healthier and more like our true self. We can do this through making time in our day, or week, for experiences where we can take time to stop and be present, focus our attention, give ourselves permission to access the flow state, let go of our ego and find our WOW once again. Often these kinds of 'childlike' experiences such as art classes, petting animals, being in the nature, being playful and spending time with others are simple but necessary in a complex and busy world. If we can do this, we might already be on our way to feeling better and saving our mind.

It needn't be hours and hours of time; research has shown that ten minutes is all you need.

You could start by pencilling 30 minutes into your diary each week for a solid dose of WOW. And then trying to micro dose during each day with mini moments on top.

FINAL WORDS

You might have picked up this book for a whole range of reasons, you might be reading now for many more. But what I, and the 15,000 children who were my inspiration, hope is; that you are well, and that you find at least one more moment of WOW today than perhaps you otherwise would without reading it.

I hope that you can remember what it feels like to be curious and want to learn, to take time to discover and try new experiences, be creative and maybe even play. I hope that you make time for those things that bring you joy, where you lose all sense of time and just for a little while forget the things that were on your mind. I hope that maybe you will take things a little slower, notice what's around you, take a deep breath and remember what is important. I hope that you try and let go of distractions and ignore some of those notifications when they flash up on the phone, I promise, everything and everyone can wait for a few moments more. I hope that when that little voice tells you that you can't do something, you tell it to be quiet and give it a go anyway.

I hope you can find something exciting and inspiring to look forward to, to try and talk to people you meet and uncover new stories and perspectives, I hope you see that nature really is the gift that keeps on giving, and that it is always there for you to enjoy and appreciate in even the smallest of ways.

Life can be tough sometimes, but there is WOW to be found, and maybe once you have found your WOW, you can help others find theirs too.

With love and WOW, Lucy

Stay in touch and Share Your WOW

T: @lucystonenow	I: @nowlucystone	Linkedin/lucystonenow
#findyourwow	I: @find.your.wow	W: thewowlab.co.uk
#wonderfield	I: @wonderfieldltd	W: wonderfield.co.uk

Chapter 17

WOW Notes & References

CHAPTER 1 – INTRODUCTION

1. Almeida, DM, Charles, ST, Mogle, J, Drewelies, J, Aldwin, CM, Spiro, A III & Gerstorf, D (2020). Charting adult development through (historically changing) daily stress processes. American Psychologist, 75(4), pp 511–524.
    Middle-aged people are more stressed in the 21st Century, BBC Science Focus Magazine https://www.sciencefocus.com/news/the-wrong-time-to-be-fifty-middle-aged-people-are-more-stressed-in-the-21st-century/
2. Permacrisis', a term describing 'an extended period of instability and insecurity', was named Collins Word of the Year 2022. It was one of several words Collins highlighted that relate to ongoing crises the UK and the world have faced and continue to face, including political instability, the war in Ukraine, climate change and the cost-of-living crisis. https://www.collinsdictionary.com/woty
3. https://www.merriam-webster.com/dictionary/wow
4. Csikszentmihalyi, Mihaly (1990). Flow: The Psychology of Optimal Experience. Journal of Leisure Research, 24(1), pp 93–94.

CHAPTER 2 – WE ARE LIVING IN A WOW-LESS WORLD

1. COVID-19: Depression, anxiety soared 25 per cent in a year, UN News https://news.un.org/en/story/2022/03/1113162
2. How common are mental health problems? 1 in 4 people will experience a mental health problem of some kind each year in England. McManus, S, Meltzer, H, Brugha, TS, Bebbington, PE & Jenkins, R (2009). Adult psychiatric morbidity in England, 2007: results of a household survey. https://digital.nhs.uk/data-and-information/publications/statistical/adult-psychiatric-morbidity-survey/adult-psychiatric-

morbidity-in-england-2007-results-of-a-household-survey
1 in 6 people report experiencing a common mental health
problem (like anxiety and depression) in any given week in England.
McManus, S, Bebbington, P, Jenkins, R & Brugha,
T (eds.) (2016). Mental health and wellbeing in
England: Adult psychiatric morbidity survey 2014.
https://webarchive.nationalarchives.gov.uk/20180328140249/http:/
digital.nhs.uk/catalogue/PUB21748

3. Simon Sinek Q & A: How Do Cell Phones Impact Our Relationships –
    YouTube
    https://www.youtube.com/watch?v=R0xYCy2eft8
    Why We Should Limit Access to Technology – YouTube
    https://www.youtube.com/watch?v=qRqkP6VtAcM
    Simon Sinek message about kids – YouTube
    https://www.youtube.com/watch?v=w3YKzZShD0A

4. TikTok trends or the pandemic? What's behind the rise in ADHD
    diagnoses, Attention deficit hyperactivity disorder, The Guardian
    https://www.theguardian.com/society/2022/jun/02/tiktok-trends-
    or-the-pandemic-whats-behind-the-rise-in-adhd-diagnoses

5. Chung, W, Jiang, S-F & Paksarian, D et al. (2019). Trends in the
    Prevalence and Incidence of Attention-Deficit/Hyperactivity Disorder
    Among Adults and Children of Different Racial and Ethnic Groups.
    JAMA Netw Open, 2(11). https://jamanetwork.com/journals/
    jamanetworkopen/fullarticle/2753787?utm_source=For_The_
    Media&utm_medium=referral&utm_campaign=ftm_links&utm_
    term=110119

6. Is modern life ruining our powers of concentration? Technology, The
    Guardian
    https://www.theguardian.com/technology/2023/jan/01/is-modern-life-
    ruining-our-powers-of-concentration?CMP=Share_iOSApp_Other

7. Abundance of information narrows our collective attention span,
    EurekAlert! https://www.eurekalert.org/news-releases/490177

8. Lorenz-Spreen, Ph, Mørch Mønsted, B, Hövel, Ph & Lehmann,
    S (2019). Accelerating dynamics of collective attention. Nature
    Communications, 10(1).

9. The World Bank (2022). Urban Development, https://www.
    worldbank.org/en/topic/urbandevelopment/overview

10. Huynh, LTM, Gasparatos, A, Su, J, Dam Lam, R, Grant, El & Fukushi,
    K (2022). Linking the nonmaterial dimensions of human-nature
    relations and human well-being through cultural ecosystem services.
    Science Advances, 8(31).

11.   Postman, Neil (2005). Amusing Ourselves to Death: Public Discourse in the Age of Show Business. Penguin Books. (Originally published in 1985.)

12.   Average adult will spend 34 years of their life looking at screens, poll claims, The Independent
https://www.independent.co.uk/life-style/fashion/news/screen-time-average-lifetime-years-phone-laptop-tv-a9508751.html

CHAPTER 3 – THE SCIENCE OF WOW

1.   'What is Awe?', Greater Good Magazine, https://greatergood.berkeley.edu/topic/awe/definition

2.   Fredrickson, Barbara (2009). Positivity. Harmony.

3.   Keltner, D & Haidt, J (2003). Approaching awe, a moral, spiritual, and aesthetic emotion. Cognition and Emotion, 17(2), pp 297–314.

4.   Anderson, CL, Monroy, M & Keltner, D (2018). Awe in nature heals: Evidence from military veterans, at-risk youth, and college students. Emotion, 18(8), 1195–1202.

5.   Rankin, K, Andrews, SE & Sweeny, K (2020). Awe-full uncertainty: Easing discomfort during waiting periods. The Journal of Positive Psychology, 15(3), 338–347.
Sense of wonderment may relieve the worry of waiting for uncertain news – ScienceDaily
https://www.sciencedaily.com/releases/2019/06/190624111532.htm

6.   Eagle, Jake & Amster, Michael (2023). The Power of Awe: Overcome Burnout & Anxiety, Ease Chronic Pain, Find Clarity & Purpose. Hachette Go.

7.   Piff, PK, Dietze, P, Feinberg, M, Stancato, DM & Keltner, D (2015). Awe, the small self, and prosocial behavior. Journal of Personality and Social Psychology, 108(6), pp 883–899.

8.   Prade, C & Saroglou, V (2016). Awe's effects on generosity and helping. The Journal of Positive Psychology, 11(5), pp 522–530.

9.   Paquette, Jonah (2020). Awestruck: How Embracing Wonder Can Make You Happier, Healthier, and More Connected. Shambhala.

10.   'The Science of Awe', Greater Good Science Center, https://ggsc.berkeley.edu/images/uploads/GGSC-JTF_White_Paper-Awe_FINAL.pdf

11.   Attention, Psychology Today United Kingdom
https://www.psychologytoday.com/gb/basics/attention

12.   Stellar, JE, Gordon, AM & Keltner, D. (2017). Self-Transcendent Emotions and Their Social Functions: Compassion, Gratitude, and Awe Bind Us to Others Through Prosociality. Emotion Review, 9(3).

13. Joye, Y & Bolderdijik, JW (2014). An exploratory study into the effects of extraordinary nature on emotions, mood, and prosociality. Frontiers in Psychology, 5: 1577

14. Stamkou, E., Brummelman, E., Dunham, R., Nikolic, M., & Keltner, D. (2023). Awe Sparks Prosociality in Children. Psychological Science, 0(0). Kids help others more after experiencing awe I BPS https://www.bps.org.uk/research-digest/kids-help-others-more-after-experiencing-awe

CHAPTER 4 – THE 15 REASONS CHILDREN FIND MEDITATION EASIER THAN ADULTS

1. Piaget's Stages: 4 Stages of Cognitive Development & Theory (positivepsychology.com) https://positivepsychology.com/piaget-stages-theory/ Human behaviour – Judgment, Britannica https://www.britannica.com/topic/human-behavior/Judgment

2. Atance, CM (2018). Future Thinking in Young Children. Current Directions in Psychological Science, 17 (4), pp 295–298.

3. McCormack, T, Burns, P, O'Connor, P, Jaroslawska, A & Caruso, EM (2019). Do children and adolescents have a future-oriented bias? A developmental study of spontaneous and cued past and future thinking. Psychological Research, 83, pp 774–787.

4. Lepper, MR et al. (2005). Intrinsic and Extrinsic Motivational Orientations in the Classroom: Age Differences and Academic Correlates. Journal of Educational Psychology, 97, 184–196. Mark Lepper: Intrinsic Motivation, Extrinsic Motivation and the Process of Learning, Bing Nursery School (stanford.edu) https://bingschool.stanford.edu/news/mark-lepper-intrinsic-motivation-extrinsic-motivation-and-process-learning

5. Mackesy, Charlie (2019). The Boy, the Mole, the Fox and the Horse. Penguin Random House UK.

6. Yet Another Reason to Exercise: It May Make You More Creative – Big Think https://bigthink.com/videos/wendy-suzuki-on-can-exercise-enhance-creativity/

7. de Bono, Edward (1999). Six Thinking Hats. Back Bay Books. (Originally published in 1985).

8. Why your toddler's 'no!' phase is so important (and how to survive it) – Today's Parent (todaysparent.com) https://www.todaysparent.com/family/parenting/why-your-toddlers-no-phase-is-so-important-and-how-to-survive-it/

9.   Not Sure What to Do With Your Life? Richard Branson Says Start by Asking These 2 Simple Questions, Inc.com
https://www.inc.com/jessica-stillman/how-to-choose-career-business-idea-richard-branson.html

10.   Lekfuangfu, WN & Odermatt, R (2022). All I have to do is dream? The role of aspirations in intergenerational mobility and well-being. European Economic Review, 148.

11.   Why Success Depends More on Personality Than Intelligence, Inc.com
https://www.inc.com/jessica-stillman/success-depends-more-on-personality-than-intelligence-new-study-shows.html

12.   Childhood aspirations are an important driver of achievement later in life, BPS
https://www.bps.org.uk/research-digest/childhood-aspirations-are-important-driver-achievement-later-life

13.   Ambitious Career Aspirations: A Double-Edged Sword, Psychology Today
https://www.psychologytoday.com/us/blog/the-economics-happiness/202208/ambitious-career-aspirations-double-edged-sword

14.   Curious children ask 73 questions each day – many of which parents can't answer, says study, The Independent
https://www.independent.co.uk/news/uk/home-news/curious-children-questions-parenting-mum-dad-google-answers-inquisitive-argos-toddlers-chad-valley-tots-town-a8089821.html

15.   The Impact of Children's Connection to Nature: A Report for the Royal Society for the Protection of Birds (RSPB) (November 2015), RSPB
https://www.rspb.org.uk/globalassets/downloads/documents/positions/education/the-impact-of-childrens-connection-to-nature.pdf

16.   Weir, K (2020) Nurtured by nature, apa.org
https://www.apa.org/monitor/2020/04/nurtured-nature

17.   Meredith, GR, Rakow, DA, Eldermire, ERB, Madsen, CG, Shelley, SP & Sachs, NA (2019). Minimum Time Dose in Nature to Positively Impact the Mental Health of College-Aged Students, and How to Measure It: A Scoping Review. Frontiers in Psychology 10.
Spending two hours a week in nature is linked to better health and well-being (theconversation.com)
https://theconversation.com/spending-two-hours-a-week-in-nature-is-linked-to-better-health-and-well-being-118653
How Much Time in Nature Is Needed to See Benefits?, Psychology Today
https://www.psychologytoday.com/us/blog/brain-waves/201906/how-much-time-in-nature-is-needed-see-benefits

Spending time in nature reduces stress, research finds, Cornell Chronicle
https://news.cornell.edu/stories/2020/02/spending-time-nature-reduces-stress-research-finds

CHAPTER 5 – WHY CHILDREN ARE THE MASTERS OF WOW

1. Bethlehem, RAI, Seidlitz, J, White, SR et al. (2022). Brain charts for the human lifespan. Nature, 604, pp 525–533.
2. 5 Types Of Brain Waves Frequencies: Gamma, Beta, Alpha, Theta, Delta – Mental Health Daily
https://mentalhealthdaily.com/2014/04/15/5-types-of-brain-waves-frequencies-gamma-beta-alpha-theta-delta/
3. Demos, John N (2005). Getting Started with Neurofeedback. WW Norton & Company.
4. The 5 Brain Waves and its Connection with Flow State, cwilsonmeloncelli.com
https://www.cwilsonmeloncelli.com/the-5-brain-waves-and-its-connection-with-flow-state/
5. Kabat-Zinn, Jon (2016). Mindfulness for Beginners: Reclaiming the Present Moment and Your Life. Boulder, Colorado: Sounds True.
6. Carson, Rachel (2017). The Sense of Wonder: A Celebration of Nature for Parents and Children. HarpPeren. (Originally published in 1955).

CHAPTER 6 – INTRODUCING THE WOW FRAMEWORK

1. Csikszentmihalyi, Mihaly (2009). Flow: The Psychology of Optimal Experience. Harper Collins.
2. Watch: NASA reveals Webb Telescope's 'deepest ever' infrared images of our universe, Euronews
https://www.euronews.com/next/2022/07/12/first-webb-telescope-image-reveals-deepest-ever-infrared-images-of-our-universe
The James Webb Space Telescope just revealed our universe anew – the view is absolutely stunning – YouTube
https://www.youtube.com/watch?v=nBDHqquK_8k
3. Yaden, DB, Haidt, J, Hood, RW, Vago, DR & Newberg, AB (2017). The Varieties of Self-Transcendent Experience. Review of General Psychology, 21(2).

CHAPTER 7 – NOW

1. Haig, Matt (2022). How to Stop Time. Canongate Book
2. Kabat-Zinn, Jon, Defining Mindfulness – Mindful
   https://www.mindful.org/jon-kabat-zinn-defining-mindfulness/
3. In the blink of an eye, MIT News, Massachusetts Institute of Technology
   https://news.mit.edu/2014/in-the-blink-of-an-eye-0116
4. Dickinson, Emily. Complete Poems. Faber & Faber (2016 Edition).
5. Wittmann, M, Giersch, A & Berkovich-Ohana, A (2019). Altered states of consciousness: With special reference to time and the self. Psych J, 8(1), pp 5–7.
6. Bailey, Chris (2020). Hyperfocus: How to Work Less to Achieve More. Pan.
7. How to Make Time Slow Down, lifehacker.com
   https://lifehacker.com/how-to-make-time-slow-down-1847212162
8. Eagleman, DM (2008). Human time perception and its illusions. Current Opinion in Neurobiology, 18(2), pp 131–136.
9. Sharif, MA, Mogilner, C & Hershfield, HE (2021). Having Too Little or Too Much Time Is Linked to Lower Subjective Well-Being. Journal of Personality and Social Psychology.
   Study links too much free time to lower sense of well-being, Psychology, The Guardian
   https://www.theguardian.com/science/2021/sep/09/study-links-too-much-free-time-to-lower-sense-of-well-being
10. Eldor, L, Fried, Y, Westman, M, Levi, AS, Shipp, AJ & Slowik, LH (2017). The experience of work stress and the context of time: analyzing the role of subjective time. Organizational Psychology Review, pp 227–249.
11. How to Start a Mindfulness Practice: A Simple Guide by Educalme – Simple Lionheart Life
   https://simplelionheartlife.com/start-a-mindfulness-practice/
12. Health Benefits of Being Outside: Improve Memory, Lower Blood Pressure, businessinsider.com
   https://www.businessinsider.com/why-spending-more-time-outside-is-healthy-2017-7?r=US&IR=T#outdoor-sessions-may-even-help-prevent-cancer-10
13. Multitasking: Switching costs, apa.org
   https://www.apa.org/topics/research/multitasking
14. Why mind-management is the solution to cleaning up your mental mess, white paper, Dr Leaf
   https://cdn.shopify.com/s/files/1/1810/9163/files/General_White_

Paper_100720_final_version.pdf?v=1602124109
How to Balance Your Brainwaves, the Different Brain Frequencies &
How – Dr Leaf (drleaf.com)lQghh_Q ^m
https://drleaf.com/blogs/news/how-to-balance-your-brainwaves-
the-different-brain-frequencies-how-they-impact-our-state-of-mind-
the-difference-between-the-mind-brain"
About the Science – Dr Leaf (drleaf.com)
https://drleaf.com/pages/research-publications

15. Chinchanachokchai, S, Duff, BRL & Sar, S (2015). The effect of
     multitasking on time perception, enjoyment, and ad evaluation.
     Computers in Human Behaviour, (45), pp 185–191.

16. How to Make Life Easier as a Highly Sensitive Person – Simple
     Lionheart Life
     https://simplelionheartlife.com/life-easier-highly-sensitive-person/

17. How to Start a Gratitude Practice to Make Your Life Better – Simple
     Lionheart Life
     https://simplelionheartlife.com/start-a-gratitude-practice/

18. 11 Unexpected Benefits of Simplifying Your Home & Life – Simple
     Lionheart Life
     https://simplelionheartlife.com/unexpected-benefits-of-simplifying/

19. Too Much Photo-Taking Can Undermine Memory: Shots – Health
     News: NPR
     https://www.npr.org/sections/health-
     shots/2021/08/05/1022041431/to-remember-the-moment-try-
     taking-fewer-photos
     Henkel, LA (2013). Point-and-Shoot Memories: The Influence
     of Taking Photos on Memory for a Museum Tour. Psychological
     Science, 25(2).
     Lurie, R & Westerman, DL (2021). Photo-Taking Impairs Memory
     on Perceptual and Conceptual Memory Tests. Journal of Applied
     Research in Memory and Cognition, 10(2), pp 289–297.

20. What Is the Memory Capacity of the Human Brain? – Scientific American
     https://www.scientificamerican.com/article/what-is-the-memory-
     capacity/

21. Wittmann, M (2018). Altered States of Consciousness: Experiences
     Out of Time and Self. The MIT Press.

22. Here's What It's Like to Begin a Meditation Practice, lifehacker.com
     https://lifehacker.com/heres-what-its-like-to-begin-a-meditation-
     practice-1846301275

23. Catherine Cook-Cottone (2015). Mindfulness and Yoga for Self-
     Regulation: A Primer for Mental Health Professionals. Springer
     Publishing.

How to make time seem like it's not speeding by, Popular Science (popsci.com)
https://www.popsci.com/diy/how-to-slow-down-time/

CHAPTER 8 – FLOW

1. Csikszentmihalyi, Mihaly (2009). Flow: The Psychology of Optimal Experience. Harper Collins.
2. Mihaly Csikszentmihalyi: Flow, the secret to happiness, TED Talk https://www.ted.com/talks/mihaly_csikszentmihalyi_flow_the_secret_to_happiness
3. Give yourself permission to be creative, Ethan Hawke – YouTube https://www.youtube.com/watch?v=WRS9Gek4V5Q
4. Nakamura, J & Csikszentmihalyi, M (2009). Flow theory and research. In SJ Lopez & CR Snyder (Eds.), Oxford Handbook of Positive Psychology, pp 195–206. Oxford University Press.
5. Leroy, S (2009). Why is it so hard to do my work? The challenge of attention residue when switching between work tasks. Organizational Behavior and Human Decision Processes, 109, pp 168–181.
6. Lacaux, C, Andrillon, Th, Bastoul, C, Idir, Y, Fonteix-Galet, A, Arnulf, I & Oudiette, D (2021). Sleep onset is a creative sweet spot. Science Advances, 7(50).
7. Losing yourself in flow state, Diane Allen, TEDxNaperville – YouTube https://www.youtube.com/watch?v=ookkfdGMHeM
8. Kotler, Steven (2014). The Rise of Superman: Decoding the Science of Ultimate Human Performance. New Harvest.
9. Csikszentmihalyi, M, Abuhamdeh, S & Nakamura, J (2005). Flow. In AJ Elliot & CS Dweck (Eds.), Handbook of Competence and Motivation (pp 598–608). Guilford Publications.
10. Fritz, BS & Avsec, A (2007). The experience of flow and subjective well-being of music students. Horizons of Psychology, 16(2), pp 5–17.
11. Myers, DG & Diener, E (1995). Who Is Happy? Psychological Science, 6(1), pp 10–19.
12. Ryff, CD, Singer, BH & Dienberg Love, G (2004). Positive health: connecting well-being with biology. Philosophical Transactions of the Royal Society London Series B Biological Sciences, 359(1449), pp 1383–1394.
13. Hanin, YL (2000). Emotions in sport. Human Kinetics.
14. Flow at Work: How to Boost Engagement in the Workplace, positivepsychology.com https://positivepsychology.com/flow-at-work/

15. Pearce, CL & Conger, JA (2003). Shared Leadership: Reframing the Hows and Whys of Leadership. Thousand Oaks, Sage Publishing.
16. Will productivity and growth return after the COVID-19 crisis?, McKinsey
     https://www.mckinsey.com/industries/public-and-social-sector/our-insights/will-productivity-and-growth-return-after-the-covid-19-crisis
17. Chirico, A, Serino, S, Cipresso, P, Gaggioli, A & Riva, G (2015). When music 'flows'. State and trait in musical performance, composition and listening: A systematic review. Frontiers in Psychology, 6, Article 906.
18. The Science of Improving Motivation at Work, positivepsychology.com
     https://positivepsychology.com/improving-motivation-at-work/
19. Burt, E & Atkinson, J (2012). The relationship between quilting and well-being. Journal of Public Health, 34(1), pp 54–59.
20. Klasen, M, Weber, R, Kircher, TT, Mathiak, KA & Mathiak, K (2012). Neural contributions to flow experience during video game playing. Social Cognitive and Affective Neuroscience, 27(4), pp 485–95.
21. Flow, USC Games Program
     https://games.usc.edu/news/flow/
22. Pilke, EM (2004). Flow experiences in information technology use. International Journal of Human-Computer Studies, 61(3), pp 347–357.
23. Csikszentmihalyi, Mihaly (1990). Flow: The Psychology of Optimal Experience. Journal of Leisure Research, 24(1), pp 93–94.
24   Pink, Daniel H (2018). Drive: The Surprising Truth About What Motivates Us. Canongate Books.
25. Sandlund, E & Norlander, T (2000). The Effects of Tai Chi Chuan Relaxation and Exercise on Stress Responses and Well-Being: An Overview of Research. International Journal of Stress Management, 7, pp 139–149.
26. van den Hout, JJJ, Davis, OC & Weggeman MCDP (2018). The Conceptualization of Team Flow. Journal of Psychology, 152(6), pp 388–423.
27. Sawyer, RK (2015). A call to action: The challenges of creative teaching and learning. Teachers College Record, 117(10), pp 1–34.
     Sawyer, Keith (2007). Group Genius: The Creative Power of Collaboration. Basic Books Inc.
28. Flow States and Creativity, Psychology Today
     https://www.psychologytoday.com/intl/blog/the-playing-field/201402/flow-states-and-creativity
29. Hjem – Slow Business, slowbusinessadventure.com
     https://www.slowbusinessadventure.com/

30. Pratt, Garry (2022). The Creativity Factor: Using the power of the outdoors to spark successful innovation. Bloomsbury Business.
31. Einaudi – Seven Days Walking – Kate Mossman, Serious
   https://serious.org.uk/einaudi-seven-days-walking-kate-mossman
32. Van Passel, P & Eggink, W (2013). Exploring the influence of self-confidence in product sketching. Proceedings of the 15th International Conference on Engineering and Product Design Education: Design Education – Growing Our Future, EPDE 2013, pp 70–75.
33. Wallace, Danny (2006). Yes Man. Ebury Press.
34. Slingerland, Edward (2014). Trying Not to Try: The Ancient Art of Effortlessness and the Surprising Power of Spontaneity. Canongate Books Ltd.

CHAPTER 9 – CULTIVATING THE CONDITIONS FOR WOW

1. Long Island Indicators, Starting Smart, chi_starting-smart.jpg (1920×1280) (rauchfoundation.org)
   https://www.rauchfoundation.org/files/7113/5853/2322/chi_starting-smart.jpg
2. Children learn more quickly than adults, neuroimaging study confirms, medicalxpress.com,
   https://medicalxpress.com/news/2022-11-children-quickly-adults.html#:~:text=%22Our%20results%20show%20that%20children%20of%20elementary%20school,during%20visual%20training%20that%20lasts%20after%20training%20ends.
   Frank, SM, Becker, M, Qi A, Geiger, P, Frank, UI, Rosedahl, LA, Malloni, WM, Sasaki, Y, Greenlee, MW & Watanabe, T (2022). Efficient learning in children with rapid GABA boosting during and after training. Current Biology, 32(23), pp 5022–5030.
3. The Kübler-Ross change curve. Kübler-Ross, E (1969). On death and dying. Macmillan.
4. Podcasts by Elizabeth Day — Elizabeth Day
   https://www.elizabethday.org/podcasts
5. 2023 marked the 110th anniversary of the publication of Swann's Way (Du côté de chez Swann), the first of seven volumes of Proust's most famous work, In Search Of Lost Time (À la recherche du temps perdu). Proust's narrator involuntarily recalls an episode from his childhood after tasting a madeleine dipped in tea.
6. In native Hawaiian culture, the sacred term 'mana' is known as spiritual energy of power and strength. It's possible for mana to be present in objects and people. For people, it's possible to gain or lose mana through the different decisions they make.

7. Haig, Matt (2022). How to Stop Time. Canongate Books.
8. Isaacson, Walter (2017). Einstein: His Life and Universe. Simon & Schuster UK.
9. Social Connectedness – an overview, ScienceDirect Topics https://www.sciencedirect.com/topics/psychology/social-connectedness
10. Huang, Z, Tarnal, V, Vlisides, Ph E, Janke, EL, McKinney, AM, Picton, P, Mashour, GA & Hudetz, AG (2021). Anterior insula regulates brain network transitions that gate conscious access. Cell Reports, 35(5).

CHAPTER 10 – THE KILLERS OF WOW: FOCUS

1. Tseng, J & Poppenk, J (220). Brain meta-state transitions demarcate thoughts across task contexts exposing the mental noise of trait neuroticism. Nature Communications, 11, 3480.
2. Amishi Jha (2021). Peak Mind: Find Your Focus, Own Your Attention, Invest 12 Minutes a Day. Piatkus Books.
3. Stress: The health epidemic of the 21st century – Thrive Global https://community.thriveglobal.com/stress-the-health-epidemic-of-the-21st-century/
4. Arnsten, AFT, Raskind, MA, Taylor, FB & Connor, DF (2015). The effects of stress exposure on prefrontal cortex: Translating basic research into successful treatments for post-traumatic stress disorder. Neurobiology of Stress, 1, pp 89–99.
5. Multitasking: Switching costs, apa.org https://www.apa.org/topics/research/multitasking
6. Why the modern world is bad for your brain, Neuroscience, The Guardian https://www.theguardian.com/science/2015/jan/18/modern-world-bad-for-brain-daniel-j-levitin-organized-mind-information-overload
7. Leroy, S (2009). Why is it so hard to do my work? The challenge of attention residue when switching between work tasks. Organizational Behavior and Human Decision Processes, 109(2), pp 168–181.
8. Newport, Cal (2016). Deep Work: Rules for Focused Success in a Distracted World. Piatkus Books.
9. Golchert, J, Smallwood, J, Jefferies, E, Seli, P, Huntenburg, JM, Liem, F, Lauckner, ME, Oligschläger, S, Bernhardt, BC, Villringer, A & Margulies, DS (2017). Individual variation in intentionality in the mind-wandering state is reflected in the integration of the default-mode, fronto-parietal, and limbic networks. Neuro Image, 146, pp 226–235.
10. Cheng, D & Wang, L (2015). Examining the Energizing Effects of Humor: The Influence of Humor on Persistence Behavior. Journal of Business Psychology, 30, pp 759–772.

11.   Paul Smith: 'I'm still blessed with enjoying every day', Fashion, The Guardian
https://www.theguardian.com/fashion/2020/oct/11/paul-smith-50th-anniversary-interview-im-still-blessed-with-enjoying-every-day
Paul on Building A Creative Environment, Paul Smith's Foundation, paulsmithsfoundation.com
https://www.paulsmithsfoundation.com/advice/building-a-creative-environment
https://www.paulsmithsfoundation.com/advice/building-a-creative-environment/my-room-childlike-inspiration
Designer Paul Smith Has the Ultimate Creative Workspace, mymodernmet.com
https://mymodernmet.com/david-baird-paul-smith-creative-space/

12.   Forster, S & Lavie, N (2009). Harnessing the wandering mind: The role of perceptual load. Cognition, 111(3), pp 345–355.

13.   Ericsson, KA, Krampe, R Th & and Tesch-Romer, C (1993). The Role of Deliberate Practice in the Acquisition of Expert Performance. Psychological Review, 100(3), pp 363–406.

14.   Ariga, A & Lleras, A (2011). Brief and rare mental 'breaks' keep you focused: Deactivation and reactivation of task goals preempt vigilance decrements. Cognition, 118(3), pp. 439–443.

15.   Gomez-Pinilla, F & Hillman, C (2013). The influence of exercise on cognitive abilities. Comprehensive Physiology, 3(1), pp 403–428.

16.   Kaplan, S & Berman, MG (2010). Directed Attention as a Common Resource for Executive Functioning and Self-Regulation. Perspectives on Psychological Science, 5(1), pp 43–57.

17.   MacLean, KA, Ferrer, E, Aichele, SR, Bridwell, DA, Zanesco, AP, Jacobs, TL, King, BG, Rosenberg, EL, Sahdra, BK, Shaver, PR, Wallace, BA, Mangun, GR & Saron, CD (2010). Intensive Meditation Training Improves Perceptual Discrimination and Sustained Attention. Psychological Science, 21(6), pp 829–839.

18.   McLellan, TM, Caldwell, JA & Lieberman, HR (2016). A review of caffeine's effects on cognitive, physical and occupational performance, Neuroscience & Biobehavioral Reviews, 71, pp 294–312.

19.   Esterman, M, Noonan, SK, Rosenberg, M & DeGutis, J (2013). In the Zone or Zoning Out? Tracking Behavioral and Neural Fluctuations During Sustained Attention. Cerebral Cortex, 23(11), pp 2712–2723.

20.   Olivers, CNL & Nieuwenhuis, S (2005). The Beneficial Effect of Concurrent Task-Irrelevant Mental Activity on Temporal Attention. Psychological Science, 16(4), pp 265–269.

21.   Resilience, Psychology Today United Kingdom
https://www.psychologytoday.com/gb/basics/resilience

22. Woolley, K & Fishbach, A (2017). Immediate Rewards Predict Adherence to Long-Term Goals. Personality and Social Psychology Bulletin, 43(2), pp 151–162.
23. Global Mindfulness Meditation Apps Market Outlook to 2027 – A USD 4,206 Million Market by 2027 – ResearchAndMarkets.com, Business Wire
   https://www.businesswire.com/news/home/20210305005147/en/Global-Mindfulness-Meditation-Apps-Market-Outlook-to-2027---A-USD-4206-Million-Market-by-2027---ResearchAndMarkets.com
24. Hari, Johann (2022). Stolen Focus: Why You Can't Pay Attention - and How to Think Deeply Again. Bloomsbury UK.

CHAPTER 11 – THE KILLERS OF WOW: EGO

1. Freud, Sigmund (1923). The Ego and the ID – PDF eBook
   https://www.sigmundfreud.net/the-ego-and-the-id-pdf-ebook.jsp
2. Jung's model of the psyche, Jung and the Ego – The SAP
   https://www.thesap.org.uk/articles-on-jungian-psychology-2/carl-gustav-jung/jungs-model-psyche/
3. Rochat, P (2003). Five levels of self-awareness as they unfold early in life. Consciousness and Cognition, 12, pp 717–731.
4. Jane Loevinger, Theory of ego development, jrank.org
   https://reference.jrank.org/psychology/Jane_Loevinger.html
5. Cohn, LD (1998). Age trends in personality development: A quantitative review. In MP Westenberg & A Blasi & LD Cohn (Eds.), Personality development: Theoretical, empirical, and clinical investigations of Loevinger's conception of ego development (pp 133–143). Lawrence Erlbaum Associates Publishers.
6. Lilgendahl, JP, Helson, R & John, OP (2013). Does ego development increase during midlife? The effects of openness and accommodative processing of difficult events. Journal of Personality, 81(4), pp 403–416.
7. Mallel (Morad), Natali, Part 1: How To Be An Adult — Kegan's Theory of Adult Development, Medium
   https://medium.com/@NataliMorad/how-to-be-an-adult-kegans-theory-of-adult-development-d63f4311b553
   Robert Kegan: The Evolution of the Self – YouTube
   https://www.youtube.com/watch?v=bhRNMj6UNYY
8. Tolle, Eckhart (2009). A New Earth. Penguin.
9. What Is Mindfulness for Children?, The Mindfulness Meditation Institute
   https://mindfulnessmeditationinstitute.org/2016/09/30/what-is-mindfulness-for-children/
10. Raise Your Emotional Awareness for More Peace and Happiness, The Mindfulness Meditation Institute

https://mindfulnessmeditationinstitute.org/2020/04/12/raise-your-emotional-awareness-for-more-peace-and-happiness/

11. What is Ego and a Possible Way to Tame it? – Thrive Global
https://community.thriveglobal.com/what-is-ego-and-a-possible-way-to-tame-it/

12. Allman, JM, Tetreault, NA, Hakeem, AY, Manaye, KF, Semendeferi, K, Erwin, JM, Park, S, Goubert, V & Hof, PR (2011). The von Economo neurons in the frontoinsular and anterior cingulate cortex. Annals New York Academy of Science, 1225, pp 59–71.

CHAPTER 12 – OTHER WOW KILLERS

1. Mental health: 'One in four adults in England has a condition' – BBC News
https://www.bbc.com/news/uk-35322354
Mental health statistics, Mental Health Foundation
https://www.mentalhealth.org.uk/explore-mental-health/statistics
Mental Health Statistics UK, Young People, YoungMinds
https://www.youngminds.org.uk/about-us/media-centre/mental-health-statistics/

CHAPTER 13 – GOOD WOW HUNTING

1. Shiota, Michelle N et al. (2007). The nature of awe: Elicitors, appraisals, and effects on self-concept. Cognition and Emotion, 21, pp 944–963.

2. How Being in Nature Can Spur Personal Growth, berkeley.edu
https://greatergood.berkeley.edu/article/item/how_being_in_nature_can_spur_personal_growth

3. Observing nature in your backyard is not dull but radically significant, Psyche Ideas
https://psyche.co/ideas/observing-nature-in-your-backyard-is-not-dull-but-radically-significant

4. Stellar, JE, John-Henderson, N, Anderson, CL, Gordon, AM, McNeil, GD & Keltner, D (2015). Positive affect and markers of inflammation: discrete positive emotions predict lower levels of inflammatory cytokines. Emotion, 15(2), pp 129–33.

5. Green and blue spaces and mental health: new evidence and perspectives for action, who.int
https://www.who.int/europe/publications/i/item/9789289055666

6. Mogan, R, Fischer, R & Bulbulia, JA (2017). To be in synchrony or not? A meta-analysis of synchrony's effects on behavior, perception, cognition and affect. Journal of Experimental Social Psychology, 72, pp 13–20.

7. Psychogenic shivers: why we get the chills when we aren't cold, Aeon Ideas
    https://aeon.co/ideas/psychogenic-shivers-why-we-get-the-chills-when-we-arent-cold
8. Carson, Rachel (2017). The Sense of Wonder: A Celebration of Nature for Parents and Children. HarpPeren. (Originally published in 1955).
9. 'We have two ears and one mouth so that we can listen twice as much as we speak.' This quote is attributed to Epictetus, a Greek philosopher who spent his youth as a slave in Rome before gaining freedom after the death of Nero, under whom he served until around 60 AD.
10. Yaden, DB, Iwry, J, Slack, KJ, Eichstaedt, JC, Zhao, Y, Vaillant, GE & Newberg, AB (2016). The overview effect: Awe and self-transcendent experience in space flight. The Psychology of Consciousness.
11. Psychedelics can have the same overview effect as a space journey, Aeon Essays
    https://aeon.co/essays/psychedelics-can-have-the-same-overview-effect-as-a-space-journey
12. SPACE (Official) – YouTube
    https://www.youtube.com/@spaceofficial
13. Exploring Earth View – YouTube
    https://www.youtube.com/watch?v=W1iQ-6KDQ2w
14. HOME, varietiescorpus
    https://www.varietiescorpus.com/
15. Chirico, A, Yaden, DB, Riva, G & Gaggioli, A (2016). The Potential of Virtual Reality for the Investigation of Awe. Frontiers in Psychology, 7.
16. Chirico, A, Cipresso, P, Yaden, DB et al. (2017). Effectiveness of Immersive Videos in Inducing Awe: An Experimental Study. Nature Scientific Reports, 7, 1218
17. https://twitter.com/scott_kerr/status/1340399932893782019
18. https://twitter.com/shannonmstirone/status/1348474763442733057
19. Ramachandran, VS (2012). The Tell-Tale Brain: Unlocking the Mystery of Human Nature. Windmill Books.
20. How the rainbow illuminates the enduring mystery of physics, Aeon Ideas
    https://aeon.co/ideas/how-the-rainbow-illuminates-the-enduring-mystery-of-physics
21. Piff, PK, Dietze, P, Feinberg, M, Stancato, DM & Keltner, D (2015). Awe, the small self, and prosocial behavior. Journal of Personality and Social Psychology, 108(6), pp 883–899.
22. Dawkins, Richard (2006). Unweaving the Rainbow: Science, Delusion and the Appetite for Wonder. Penguin.

23. Keltner, D & Haidt, J (2003). Approaching awe, a moral, spiritual, and aesthetic emotion. Cognition & Emotion, 17(2), pp 297–314.
24. Sturm, VE, Datta, S, Roy, ARK, Sible, IJ, Kosik, EL, Veziris, CR, Chow, TE, Morris, NA, Neuhaus, J, Kramer, JH, Miller, BL, Holley, SR & Keltner, D (2022). Big smile, small self: Awe walks promote prosocial positive emotions in older adults. Emotion, 22(5), pp 1044–1058.
25. Awe Walk, Practice, Greater Good in Action, berkeley.edu https://ggia.berkeley.edu/practice/awe_walk

CHAPTER 14 – FIND YOUR OWN WOW

1. Rauch, Jonathan (2019). The Happiness Curve: Why Life Gets Better After Midlife. Green Tree
2. This chart predicts the age at which you'll be happiest, World Economic Forum (weforum.org) https://www.weforum.org/agenda/2017/08/youll-probably-have-a-midlife-happiness-crisis-heres-why
3. Dylan Moran – The 4 Stages of Life, Universal Comedy – YouTube https://www.youtube.com/watch?v=8YNlzpxcBe8
4. Mogi, Ken (2018). The Little Book of Ikigai: The secret Japanese way to live a happy and long life. Quercus.

CHAPTER 15 – THE NEW WOW ORDER

1. Gabriel, S, Valenti, J, Naragon-Gainey, K & Young, AF (2017). The psychological importance of collective assembly: Development and validation of the Tendency for Effervescent Assembly Measure (TEAM). Psychological Assessment, 29(11), pp 1349–1362.
Stories of Impact: Collective Effervescence with Or Taicher, Michal Shahaf, Ben Yaffet and Dr. Shira Gabriel, libsyn.com https://storiesofimpact.libsyn.com/collective-effervescence-with-or-taicher-michal-shahaf-ben-yaffet-and-dr-shira-gabriel
Tools for Human Flourishing: Collective Effervescence – With Koolulam & Shira Gabriel, Templeton World Charity Foundation, Inc. https://www.templetonworldcharity.org/blog/tools-human-flourishing-collective-effervescence-koolulam-shira-gabriel
2. The Global Decline of Religion, foreignaffairs.com https://www.foreignaffairs.com/articles/world/2020-08-11/religion-giving-god?fbclid=IwAR0ic8NhBeOWKCpge8qcG-g4u-JCV8i1qIPkUgQj1dxjoR786S3NZIRsEFU

3.   Frankl, Viktor E (2004). Man's Search For Meaning: The classic tribute to hope from the Holocaust. Rider. (Originally published in 1946).

CHAPTER 16 – CAN WOW REALLY SAVE YOUR MIND?

1.   How the brain responds to surprising events, MIT News, Massachusetts Institute of Technology
      https://news.mit.edu/2022/noradrenaline-brain-surprise-0601
2.   The Temporal Lobe: The Center of Memory and Emotions, exploringyourmind.com
      https://exploringyourmind.com/the-temporal-lobe-the-center-of-memory-and-emotions/
3.   Dopamine vs. Serotonin: Depression, Digestion, Sleep, and More, healthline.com
      https://www.healthline.com/health/dopamine-vs-serotonin
4.   Serotonin: Functions, Normal Range, Side Effects, and More, healthline.com https://www.healthline.com/health/mental-health/serotonin
5.   Love Hormone: What Is Oxytocin and What Are Its Effects?, healthline.com
      https://www.healthline.com/health/love-hormone
6.   Endorphins: Functions, Levels, and Natural Boosts, healthline.com
      https://www.healthline.com/health/endorphins
7.   What Are the Benefits of Sunlight?, healthline.com
      https://www.healthline.com/health/depression/benefits-sunlight
8.   van der Rhee, HJ, de Vries, E & Coebergh, JW (2016). Regular sun exposure benefits health. Medical Hypotheses, 97, pp 34–37.
9.   Exercise: The Top 10 Benefits of Regular Physical Activity, healthline.com
      https://www.healthline.com/nutrition/10-benefits-of-exercise
10.   Runner's High: What It Is, How You Get It, and Other Benefits, healthline.com
      https://www.healthline.com/health/runners-high
11.   Yorks, DM, Frothingham, CA, Schuenke, MD (2017). Effects of Group Fitness Classes on Stress and Quality of Life of Medical Students. The Journal of the American Osteopathic Association, 117(11).
12.   Anxiety Disorders: Causes, Types, Symptoms & Treatments, healthline.com
      https://www.healthline.com/health/anxiety
13.   Why You Should Get (and Give) More Hugs, healthline.com
      https://www.healthline.com/health/hugging-benefits
14.   Oxytocin: The love hormone – Harvard Health
      https://www.health.harvard.edu/mind-and-mood/oxytocin-the-love-hormone

15. Ferreri, L, Mas-Herrero, E, Zatorre, R & Rodriguez-Fornells, A (2019). Dopamine modulates the reward experiences elicited by music. PNAS, 116(9), pp 3793–3798.
16. Pascolo, PB & Bucci, A (2019). Mirror Neurons in the Macaque Monkey: A Critical Review. Critical Reviews in Biomedical Engineering, 47(6), pp 507–513.
17. Cross, ES, Kraemer, DJ, Hamilton, AFDC, Kelley, WM & Grafton, ST (2009). Sensitivity of the action observation network to physical and observational learning. Cerebral Cortex, 19, pp 315–326.
18. Wondra, JD & Ellsworth, Ph C (2015). An Appraisal Theory of Empathy and Other Vicarious Emotional Experiences. Psychological Review, 122(3), pp 411–428.
19. Brandner, P, Güroğlu, B & Crone, EA (2020). I am happy for us: Neural processing of vicarious joy when winning for parents versus strangers. Cognitive, Affective & Behavioral Neuroscience, 20, pp 1309–1322.
20. Batson, CD, Batson, JG, Slingsby, JK, Harrell, KL, Peekna, HM & Todd, RM (1991). Empathic joy and the empathy-altruism hypothesis. Journal of Personality and Social Psychology, 61(3), 413–426.
21. Andreoni, J (1990). Impure altruism and donations to public goods: A theory of warm-glow giving. The Economic Journal, 100, pp 464–477.
22. Schnell, K, Bluschke, S, Konradt, B & Walter, H (2011). Functional relations of empathy and mentalizing: An fMRI study on the neural basis of cognitive empathy. NeuroImage, 54(2), pp 1743–1754.
23. Vanstone: Why can sports leave us so out of sorts?, Regina Leader Post
https://leaderpost.com/sports/rob-vanstone-why-can-sports-leave-us-so-out-of-sorts
24. Steve Barclay urged to extend green social prescribing programme, UK Healthcare News (nationalhealthexecutive.com)
https://www.nationalhealthexecutive.com/articles/steve-barclay-urged-extend-green-social-prescribing-programme